WEIGHT TRAINING

About the Author

Dr. Rasch purchased his first barbell in 1926, and has been involved with this form of training ever since. He holds an A.B. (Anthropology) degree from California State University Dominguez Hills and A.B. (Physical Education), M.A. (Physical Education), M.Ed., and Ph.D. (Physical Education) degrees from the University of Southern California.

After World War II service in the Navy, from which he has since retired as a Lieutenant Commander, Dr. Rasch has worked as a Corrective Therapist at the Veterans Administration Hospital, Los Angeles, Director of the Biokinetics Research Laboratory, California College of Medicine, and Chief, Physiology Division Naval Medical Field Research Laboratory, Camp Lejeune, N.C., where he also served as physiologist for the U.S. Marine Corps Physical Fitness Academy, Quantico, Va. He is now retired.

He is author or coauthor of several books and well over one hundred articles. Dr. Rasch is a Fellow of the American College of Sports Medicine, a Fellow of the Research Consortium of the American Association for Health, Physical Education, Recreation, and Dance, an Honorary Life Member of the Royal Air Force School of Physical Training, and an Associate Editor of the **National Strength Coaches Association Journal.** He is listed in **Who's Who in Science.**

WEIGHT TRAINING

Fifth Edition

Philip J. Rasch

Formerly Chief Physiology Division,
Naval Medical Field Research Laboratory,
Camp LeJeune, North Carolina

Honorary Life Member,
Royal Air Force School of Physical Training

wcb

Wm. C. Brown Publishers
Dubuque, Iowa

Consulting Editor
Physical Education
Aileene Lockhart
Texas Woman's University

Cover photo © Bob Coyle

Library of Congress Catalog Card Number: 88–43259

ISBN 0–697–10417–6

Printed in the United States of America by Wm. C. Brown Publishers
2460 Kerper Boulevard, Dubuque, IA 52001

10   9   8   7   6   5   4

contents

Preface

Since the appearance in 1982 of the Fourth Edition of this booklet there has been a veritable explosion of mechanical devices designed to replace the use of free weights. These are expensive and there is little evidence they are any more effective in developing the body than are free weights. Accordingly, very little space has been devoted to them in this the Fifth Edition. The possibility that one or another of these pieces of apparatus, or of others yet to be invented, may prove to be a superior means of training must be judged by a program of comparative testing by unbiased scientists. For the present ask anyone trying to convince you of their superiority to show you the studies upon which he bases his statements. A convenient guide to investigations in this field is the annual *Completed Research,* published by the American Alliance for Health, Physical Education, Recreation and Dance.

The major problem in weight training continues to be the abuse of drugs. Five weight lifters were included among the ten competitors so far found guilty of their use during the 1988 Seoul Olympics. One result was that Richard Pound, Canadian vice president of the International Olympic Committee, announced that he would seek the suspension of weight lifting from the Olympics. It is not likely that this move will receive much support, but the fact that such a proposal could even be contemplated is an indication of the seriousness of the problem.

One recent study reported that the use of drugs is widespread among young men who desire to display a muscular body but who do not want to undertake the arduous training necessary to develop it through exercise. It should not be necessary to warn readers of this booklet of the dangers of attempting such an apparent shortcut.

Insofar as they are known, the scientific facts underlying the practice of weight training have been set forth in this text. Improvement in physique can be accompanied by improvements in health, sports performance, work performance, psychological attitude, self-confidence, and many other desirable qualities, but what one gets out of it depends largely on what one puts into it. Inevitably there will be periods of discouragement when one's best efforts seem to fail to produce gains. Be sure your goals are reasonable and persist in your training. We cannot all be Mr. or Miss Americas.

Often such dilemmas are best overcome by taking a short vacation and returning to the program with renewed enthusiasm. Almost certainly you will make further progress toward achieving your goals.

Bill Pearl. (Photo by Chris Lund, courtesy of Bill Pearl.)

This picture of Bill Pearl shows him as he appeared on his 56th birthday. (Photo by Chris Lund, courtesy of Bill Pearl.) Beside being living proof that continued vigorous training will enable a person to retain his youthful physique, Pearl is one of the most respected and admired body builders of our day. Experts say his triceps in his prime have never been equaled.

Introduction to Weight Training

1

Weight training, more formally known as progressive resistance exercise, may be divided into five subdivisions:

Weight Lifters   This group comprises competitive lifters interested mainly in the two Olympic lifts: the two-hand snatch and the two-hand clean and jerk. Technical rules, a register of world records, and medical studies are functions of the International Weightlifting Federation (Federation Halterophile Internationale), whose meetings are usually held in conjunction with the Olympic Games. Ordinarily these athletes employ maximal or near-maximal poundages and do not perform over three repetitions of a given exercise at a time. They may perform single repetitions with rest periods between.

Power Lifters   Power lifters are concerned almost exclusively with the development of brute strength. They compete in the three power lifts—squat, bench press, and dead lift, contested in that order—under rules established by the International Powerlift Federation. On occasion, the curl or some other form of lifting may be added, and the event is then billed as an Odd Lifts Meet. The training program of power lifters tends toward the use of extremely heavy weights with low repetitions and a large number of sets.

Body Builders   Physical contestants are more interested in developing massive musculature and great definition than exceptional strength. They tend to perform several sets of an exercise with a high number of repetitions in each set in an effort to engorge the muscle tissue with blood. Since the relationship between limb girth and strength is relatively small, body builders are not always as strong as their muscle size might lead the observer to expect, and they often lack cardiorespiratory endurance.

Athletes   Weight training has become extremely popular as a method of preparation for participation in athletics, particularly among weight throwers, football players and swimmers. They practice special programs designed by their coaches to develop strength in the movements specific to their sport. These coaches have formed a professional organization known as the National Strength and Conditioning Association.

Patients   Progressive resistance exercises under medical supervision are prescribed to meet a patient's individual needs and are often concentrated on the afflicted area rather than over the entire body. In many cases, a bodybuilder routine is followed, as the restoration to normal appearance of an atrophied limb (the so-called cosmetic effect) is often of greater concern to the sufferer than regaining normal strength.

Of the foregoing, weight lifting, power lifting, and rehabilitation procedures fall outside the scope of this book and will not be considered further. The physiologic principles discussed on the following pages are, however, as valid for those engaged in these activities as for any other group.

Physiologic Principles of Weight Training

The bones are, in effect, a system of articulated levers which are moved by the skeletal muscles. Muscles may be regarded as machines which store chemical energy and convert it to mechanical work in response to impulses conducted by the nervous system. There are approximately 434 muscles, making up about 40 to 45 percent of the body weight, but only about 75 pairs are involved in the general movements of the body. A muscle consists of a large number of cells filled with a liquid protein solution called sarcoplasm. Running through this material are elements called myofibrils. These are the units actually responsible for the process of contraction. The most popular theory is that the myofibrils contain filaments which slide past each other when a muscle contracts or elongates. Skeletal muscle contains two types of fibers—red, adapted to slow, prolonged contractions, and white, designed for fast contractions.

There are three types of muscular contraction, each of which has been used as the basis for training systems.

Isotonic   The muscle actually shortens and moves a load, such as a barbell or dumbbell through a distance, thus accomplishing a certain amount of work. Such contractions are also said to be concentric. In practice the weight that can be handled is limited to that which can be moved through the weakest point in the range of motion of a joint.

Isokinetic exercise   is a modification of isotonic exercise. It utilizes a machine which controls the speed of the movement. This prevents the dissipation of muscular energy in acceleration, and provides resistance proportional to the input of muscular force and the alterations in skeletal levers throughout the range of motion. In simpler language, it compensates for the variations in the muscle force which can be developed at various angles of a joint, and provides maximal resistance at any angle. This apparatus is seldom seen in gymnasia at the present time, but many have equipment somewhat similar in principle, but which does not incorporate the speed control mechanism. These are known as **variable resistance machines.**

Isokinetic machines appear to present no advantages over traditional isotonic methods.[1] From a functional standpoint, the relationship of such apparatus to natural movements has not been determined.

Isometric   The muscle is unable to move the load, such as a fixed bar, so that apparently no joint movement takes place. The muscle does not visibly shorten, and technically, no work is accomplished even though the muscle is subjected to great stress. This is known as static contraction. The value of this type of exercise has been reviewed elsewhere.[2]

Lengthening The load forces the contracted muscle to extend, as when a barbell is taken from supports and slowly lowered. This is also a form of isotonic contraction and is known as eccentric contraction in order to differentiate it from concentric movements. It is commonly termed negative exercise by weight trainers. In practice it is utilized every time a weight is lowered in a controlled manner during isotonic exercise.

These explanations are somewhat oversimplified and are not completely accurate from the standpoint of muscle physiology. A consideration of the details would take us far astray, however, and for our purposes it is satisfactory to act as if they were correct.

The amount of force a muscle can exert depends on the number and size of its myofibrils. It has been believed for nearly seventy-five years that the number of fibrils cannot be increased by exercise and that growth in muscular size (hypertrophy) results from increases in the sizes of the muscle fibers. However, recent studies have raised some question about the correctness of the belief that the number of fibrils cannot change.[3]

Contrary to popular belief, the relationship between limb girth and strength is relatively small. What actually determines the force that can be exerted by a muscle? Why does a muscle increase in size during exercise?

When a muscle is exercised, the material enclosing the cell (*sarcolemma*) becomes thickened and toughened, and the amount of connective tissue increases. There is also an increase in certain chemical constituents of the cell, the blood flow, and the blood pressure. The capillaries (tiny blood vessels) open and dilate, and fluid is attracted from the blood into the tissue spaces. All of this may increase the weight of the muscle by as much as 20 percent. During the rest period following exercise there will be a reduction in the muscle's size, but it will tend to remain somewhat larger than it was before exercise. If the muscle is worked regularly, there will be a permanent increase in the number of capillaries, the ability of the muscle to assimilate nutritive materials will improve, and the size and functional power of the cells will increase.

In general, biochemical studies endeavoring to explain the changes resulting in muscle from training have not been very enlightening. Recent attention has tended to center on the role of the brain and spinal cord. It has been suggested that the power of a muscle depends upon the number of motor units the nervous system is able to excite in a muscle. It is possible some of them are more easily triggered than are others, and those hardest to arouse can perhaps be brought under voluntary control only as a result of maximal or near-maximal efforts. Strength may be more neurological and psychological than physical.

Rather obviously, the foregoing changes do not appear at the same rate or to the same extent in all individuals, even when they are following identical training programs. Some individuals are what the body builders call "easy gainers" (fig. 1.1); others are "hard gainers." Some people have more fibers in a given

Figure 1.1
Bill Trumbo. Development like this requires that a man have certain natural advantages to begin with and be an "easy gainer" in addition. Trumbo's chest measurement is about 51 inches. Despite the claims in advertisements, relatively few individuals can achieve Trumbo's result. (Photograph courtesy of Photographic Services, Inc.)

muscle, more advantageous muscle composition, better muscle leverage, or even muscles which others lack. Even so, these differences in response to physical activity are not fully understood. By the same token, we have not discovered all the laws underlying successful training. Exercise physiologists, however, are quite confident of the following principles:

1. Strength, endurance, and muscle size increase, within limits, in response to repetitive exercise against progressively increased resistance. This is known as the **overload principle** and requires a psychological approach committed to all-out efforts. The **overload principle** is the basis of all programs of weight training.
2. For each individual there is an optimal pattern for such exercises. This involves the **intensity** of the stress imposed on the muscle, the **duration** of the training periods, and the **frequency** of the workouts. It is possible that the relative influence of each changes as the training progresses.
3. Of the three variables in a training program, **intensity** is the most important. There is some evidence that the amount of fatigue a muscle undergoes is important in determining the training effect.
4. The critical factor is the amount of stress placed upon the body during the given training time. More formally expressed, this is the **SAID Principle**— exercise induces **specific adaptations to imposed demands.** Improvements in strength and oxygen capacity depend on the work performed, not on the type of equipment used.
5. Exercises which do not involve overloading the body systems have relatively little effect upon performance ability.
6. Muscles forced to perform repeated contractions at progressively increased loads respond by hypertrophying as well as by increasing their strength, but the relationship between hypertrophy and strength is not clear.

7. Different muscles may respond better to different programs of exericse.
8. As muscular strength increases, **trainability** (ability to respond to repeated contractions of a given force, duration, and frequency by the development of greater strength) decreases.
9. Muscles contain two types of fibers: slow twitch (red) and fast twitch (white). The ratio between the two is a hereditary matter and cannot be altered by training. The top competitors of each sport often have a "mix" especially suited to that particular activity. To this extent, champion athletes are born, not made. Weight trainers are now experimenting with programs which include brief, high-intensity exercises to train the white fibers, and prolonged, low-intensity exercises to train the red fibers.
10. Training is **specific**. That is, training for one activity is beneficial for another activity only to the extent that the two have specific motor patterns in common. The implications of this principle are that specialized training is a necessary part of the preparation for success in most sports. The speed of exercise movements may itself be a specific.
11. **Principle of Reversibility.** The weight trainer who ceases to train will gradually lose the strength and hypertrophy acquired by that training. Strength is said to be lost at a rate of one-third that of its acquisition.
12. One of the keys to balanced development is to include exercises for the antagonists in each workout—for instance, bent over rowing motions with bench presses, leg curls with squats, etc.

What is the principle on which any increase in strength depends? How important is your choice of the type of progressive resistance training?

Attention is especially directed to principles 2, 3, and 4. It will be shown later that research studies have generally failed to demonstrate significant differences in the results obtained from various programs and types of overloading equipment. Apparently it matters comparatively little whether one sort of progressive resistance training or another is used so long as the intensity in particular, and duration and frequency to a lesser degree, apply an equivalent amount of stress in each case.

We do not know as much as we should like to about the best methods of invoking the overload principle, but the physiologists have several hints to offer the weight trainer.

1. A muscle is in position to exert its greatest force when it is somewhat stretched. Each movement should begin from a position in which the joint is fully extended and end with it fully contracted.
2. Mechanical efficiency is greatest at about one-fifth of the maximal speed.
3. To permit repetitions, the resistance must be sufficiently large to demand a greater-than-normal effort, but small enough to require a less-than-maximal effort.
4. There is some evidence that exercise is more effective if done to a definite rhythm.
5. Short, frequent rest pauses should be observed to prevent the muscle from becoming fatigued early in the training session. This gives the heart a chance

to drive blood through the muscle, rinsing out waste products and bringing in food and oxygen. The result is a greater work output even though less time is spent in actually moving the weights. In a normal training routine it appears to make no difference in strength gains if the rest pause is 30 seconds, 2.5 minutes, or 8 minutes.[4]

The serious weight trainer should be alert for four possible developments in his field:

a. Since different muscles may respond better to different programs of exercise, we may see the development of separate routines for various body parts.
b. The validity of the second principle is not beyond question. There is evidence that mechanical efficiency is greater when flexion of a muscle is immediately followed by its extension. This is termed "elastic rebound." Rebound methods of training may receive more attention in the future than they have in the past. Such exercises are termed "plyometrics" by weight trainers and "stretch-shortening" by exercise physiologists.
c. In the future, progressive resistance training programs may include a mix of concentric, eccentric, and isometric exercises. Soviet researchers recommend weight lifters follow a program consisting of 75% concentric, 15% eccentric, and 10% isometric work (fig. 1.2).
d. Soviet researchers believe the best results are achieved when there is a mixture of fast, moderate, and slow tempos in executing the exercises.

Is the position of this elbow joint appropriate for beginning an exercise movement? Would it be correct if the elbow were flexed at a right angle? At about what speed of movement is mechanical efficiency greatest?

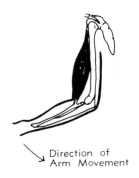

Direction of
Arm Movement

Strength and Power

A great deal of confusion exists in the popular literature dealing with weight training because uninformed writers often use the terms "strength" and "power" as though they were interchangeable. They have separate and distinct meanings. Strength refers to the ability to produce or resist a force. Power refers to the **rate** at which work is done and is determined by dividing the work done by the time taken to do it. Power would be greater if a given weight were lifted in a shorter

Figure 1.2
Igor Nikitin, USSR, silver medal winner 220 lb. class 1980 Olympic Games. This is one of the finest photographs of back musculature I have ever seen. The depth of the trapezius and erector spinae muscles is amazing. If Nikitin's development is a product of the Soviet training methods described on page 6, they must be treated with respect. (Photo by Everill Taggart.)

time, although it would be said that the man's strength was unchanged. Power lifting, for example, is an improper term because no attention is paid to the time required to complete a lift. You must keep this distinction between the two terms in mind or you will be in danger of being either misinformed or confused by much of what you read. Remember, it is power that is important to the athlete.

The accurate definition of the term "power" and its meaning in a popular magazine devoted to weight lifting may differ. What is the correct definition, and to what does the word refer as it is commonly misused?

Health Spas

Many adults enroll in commercial gymnasia called health spas. These institutions are often controversial with reference to their business practices and in regard to the qualifications of their instructors. Many of these concerns are oriented toward sales rather than service. They are often ephemeral. The fact that 75 percent of their new members use the facilities for only about three months before dropping out signals a need for caution before signing a long-term contract. It is recommended that anyone considering buying a membership should first visit a library and read the Federal Trade Commission's Report *Health Spas*. This may save the reader disappointment and expense.

Mechanical Aids

The apparatus in commercial gymnasia often includes belt vibrators, rollers, and other effortless "spot reducers." The claims of the hucksters notwithstanding, the bulk of the evidence indicates that these machines have no value for that purpose. There is no such thing as spot reducing which can result from massage or vibrating machines of any type. The fat content present in animal tissue is unchanged even when subjected to massage forceful enough to produce multiple hemorrhages. Mechanical vibrators are equally useless for this purpose. Physiologists know of no mechanism of fat mobilization which supports the concept that they would be helpful.

Saunas

In recent years commercial gymnasia have tended to emphasize saunas when advertising their facilities. Some years ago the alleged benefits of these baths were the subject of a good deal of scientific investigation. It was shown that they raised the body temperature about 1° C. and considerably increased sweat production and pulse rate. These baths may have value as a cleansing procedure, but no known physiologic or medical benefits result from their use. The sauna should be avoided in cases of acute infections, hypertension, diabetes, acute kidney involvement, and eye involvements. Some physicians believe use of a sauna may be dangerous to a large segment of the population. Elderly persons and pregnant women should probably refrain from using it.

A sauna should not be visited immediately after a heavy meal. Any occurrence of breathlessness, dizziness, headache, or palpitation of the heart should be regarded as a warning sign and the bath should be terminated. The increased sweat rate, of course, results in a transient weight loss; users should not delude themselves that this represents any permanent reduction of body weight.

Myths About Weight Training

The term "muscle-bound" refers to a limitation of motion which occasionally results when a movement requiring less than the normal range of motion is constantly practiced. Bicycle riders sometimes become muscle-bound in the legs, with the result that they cannot extend the lower leg properly when trying to kick a football. Such restriction of movement is evidence of an improper training program. It is, however, true that the sheer bulk of muscle may reduce the range of a given movement and that muscular men in general have less joint mobility than do slender types. Further, each type of athletics tends to reflect a flexibility pattern peculiar to itself. Thus, swimmers may exceed weight trainers in the flexibility of certain joints, but be exceeded in others by the weight trainers. Apparently ranges of movement tend to become fixed within limits producing the best performance in the activity involved.

There is no evidence that practice of a proper weight-training program will make a person slow or will adversely affect coordination. If anything, the opposite is true, but there seems to be a limit after which further increases in strength are not accompanied by improvement in speed.

One of the most venerable myths about weight training is that it is "bad for your heart," in what way it is bad never being explained. This fable should have been laid to rest in 1959, when Etzenhouser and his colleagues[5] examined twenty-six weight lifters and found their hearts were all within normal physiological limits. It still crops up occasionally, but subsequent studies right down to the quite recent present[6] support the findings of Etzenhouser et al.

There are many misconceptions about terminology and practices related to exercise and fitness. Can you identify erroneous beliefs in relation to power, spot reducing, and sauna?

Weight Training and Physical Fitness

Having said this much, the fact must be added that although weight training is unequaled as a means of developing strength, this does not mean it is a perfect exercise. A number of studies have shown that its practice results in very little improvement in cardiorespiratory function. In tests of work capacity, weight lifters have been found to be no better than the untrained. If the weight trainer desires to be fit as well as strong, it will be necessary to add a good deal of running to the regimen—perhaps something on the order of the aerobics programs which have been so popular during the last few years. In any event, the activity must be vigorous enough so that the heart rate for healthy young persons exceeds 150 beats per minute, or no training effect will result. Weight training exercises require an oxygen consumption similar to that found in walking on a flat surface at 4 mph. This is a minimal level for improving cardiorespiratory fitness. The working of the principle of specificity of training make it impossible to simultaneously train for maximal strength and maximal endurance.[7]

Sleep

Sleep conserves and restores energy. Heavy consumption of salt, refined sugars, and caffeine-containing drinks such as coffee may cause insomnia in sensitive persons. There is a good deal of evidence that smokers experience a poorer quality of sleep than do nonsmokers. The result may be that fatigue builds up and performance decreases. Sleep deprivation results in reduced performance, but how much sleep an athlete can lose before performance is affected, or how much sleep is required for optimal performance, is not clear. Possibly that is determined by age, sex, and physical fitness. What little evidence is available suggests that about seven or eight hours a night is optimal. The time of day at which one exercises has no known effect on the results, but the weight trainer may find it difficult to get to sleep if a vigorous workout is taken just before going to bed. An exerciser should allow an hour or so for the body systems to return to normal before retiring.

If a person is strong, is the individual fit? What significance does the answer have for a person who "exercises for health?"

References

1. Gettman, Larry R., *et al.* 1980. Physiologic changes after 20 weeks of isotonic vs. isokinetic circuit training. *Journal of Sports Medicine* 20:265–74.
2. Rasch, Philip J. Isometric Exercise and Gains of Muscle Strength. In Roy Shephard, ed. *Frontiers of Fitness.* Springfield, Ill.: Charles C Thomas, 1971, 98–111.
3. Gonyea, William J. 1980. Role of exercise in inducing increases in skeletal muscle fiber number. *Journal of Applied Physiology* 48:421–26.
4. Berkowitz, Marvin S. 1978. Effects of varying rest intervals between sets on the acquisition of muscular strength. Unpublished M.S. Thesis, Pennsylvania State University.
5. Etzenhouser, Russell. 1959. Electrocardiograms of Weight Lifters. *Journal of the Kansas Medical Society* 60:121–25.
6. Corser, T., *et al.* 1968. Cardiac and other muscular responses to heavy weight lifting. *Journal of Physiology* 19:66p–67p.
7. Hickson, Robert C. 1980. Interference of Strength Development by Simultaneously Training for Strength and Endurance. *European Journal of Applied Physiology,* 45:255–63.

Diet and Nutrition

2

Probably nothing else connected with weight training is as confusing to the novice as diet and nutrition. Smith complains that athletes "are bombarded with threatening information by a host of nutrition quacks, fad diets, cultists, charlatans, and hucksters of all kinds."[1] Bodybuilders in particular have a tendency to be faddish in their diet and to consume great quantities of "health foods," "organically grown foods," proteins, vitamins, and other dietary supplements. It is, of course, of great financial advantage to those selling such products to promote belief in the need for them—a point which should be kept in mind when reading the magazines devoted to weight training.

The facts are that chemically and organically grown* foods do not differ in taste or chemical analysis. Vitamins from natural sources have no nutritional superiority over synthetic vitamins. Most of the articles on nutrition published in weight training magazines are strictly anecdotal. Experimental research, including the use of a control group and statistical evaluation, is almost never cited. It is generally impossible to determine from such articles whether the supplement used had any effect at all.

How can the validity of such articles be estimated? When in doubt, ask the following questions.

1. Does the author hold a degree in nutrition, biochemistry, physiology, or another appropriate field from an accredited college or university?
2. Does the author belong to the American Dietetic Association or other appropriate professional organizations?
3. Does the author cite the controlled research studies on which the advice is based?
4. Does the author use recognized methods of nutritional assessment, such as skinfold thickness and appropriate laboratory tests, and subject these results to appropriate statistical analysis?
5. Does the author have a vested interest in the product which he extolls?

If any of the answers to questions 1 through 4 are negative and/or that to question 5 is positive, the need for an attitude of enlightened skepticism is strongly indicated.

In 1985, the Dietary Guidelines Advisory Committee of the U.S. Department of Agriculture recommended that the American diet include a variety of foods drawn from the following groups.

---

*That is, from soil on which no chemical fertilizer or pesticide has been used. In any event, the quantity so grown is said to be less than 25 percent of that sold in "organic" stores!

Fruits

Vegetables

Whole grain and enriched breads, cereals, and other products made from grain

Milk, cheese, yogurt, and other products made from milk

Meats, poultry, fish, eggs, and dry beans and peas

Some experts believe that this advice is incomplete in that it does not provide against inclusion of excessive saturated fat or cholesterol in meals, certain essential vitamins and minerals are not included, the need for water is not mentioned, and the role of fiber is not stressed. It is evident that much more research is needed before nutrition recommendations can be considered to be truly scientific.

There are, however, six essential nutrients: proteins, carbohydrates, fats, vitamins, minerals, and water. Of these, exercise increases the need for energy-supplying substances and for water to replace that lost in sweat. The food intake of Olympic weight lifters averages around 3,900 kilocalories per day. This amount should be more than ample for the weight trainers unless they are on a massive program designed to increase body weight. The major portion should be carbohydrates, as it is from this source that the body derives most of its energy. Fats also serve as an important source of energy, but work efficiency is lower on a high-fat diet than on a high-carbohydrate intake, and some nutritionists believe a diet high in fat may increase the risk of cancer. Protein is necessary for maintenance and growth of the tissues; in the United States, the average diet appears to be more than adequate in this respect.

What has research revealed in regard to organically grown foods and vitamin supplements?

In one study it was found that the diet followed by the body-builders made a startling contrast with the Recommended Dietary Allowances.[2] A comparison is shown in table 2.1.

American weight trainers are notorious for the huge amounts of protein and amino acid supplements they ingest, in spite of the fact that independent investigators have reported again and again that no benefits result from the use of protein supplements or excess vitamins when the subjects are subsisting on a normal American diet.[3] A few years ago the Federal Trade Commission considered adopting a trade regulation rule which would prohibit any representation that "Protein is used . . . in greater than normal amounts by strenuous physical activity of any kind" or that "Use of a protein supplement can improve or increase the level of performance of athletes or strenuous physical labor by increasing strength, endurance, vitality, and vigor of muscle tissue."[4]

One problem is that protein is composed of amino acids. These are converted to urea and excreted in the urine. This requires water and may aggravate the dehydration commonly practiced by athletes "making weight." Also, too much protein in the diet may leave an acid residue which imposes an extra load on the kidneys and accelerates the normal loss of kidney function that occurs with age.

If one enjoys drinking milk and tolerates it well, it is an excellent source of protein and other nutrients. The other side of the story is that it is also high in fat. Furthermore, a high percentage of our population finds that it gives them

Table 2.1 Recommended Dietary Guidelines and Body Builders' Diet

Nutrient	RDG Average American	RDG Athletes in Training	Actual Body Builders' Diet
Protein	15%	10–20%	85%
Carbohydrate	42%	50–55%	5% or less
Fat	43%	30–35%	10%

Note. The body builders' diet contains two to three times the average American cholesterol consumption per day.

From Diana L. Spitler, *et al.*, "Body Composition and Maximal Aerobic Capacity of Body Builders" in *Journal of Sports Medicine and Physical Fitness*, 20:181–180, 1980. Copyright © 1980 J. B. Lippincott, Co., Philadelphia, PA.

flatulence, cramps, and diarrhea. Inability to use milk is especially high among those of American Indian, Oriental, African, and Greek descent. This seems to be related to the fact that their ancestors did not use it and thus failed to develop the enzyme called lactose which is necessary for its digestion. If one's body does not tolerate milk, this should cause no worry—simply do not drink it. Some nutritionists recommend the use of low-fat milk.

There are no miracle foods. Yogurt, blackstrap molasses, brewer's yeast, and similar substances are wholesome and nutritious, but no more so than other products which are usually much less expensive. There is no foundation for the claim that soil depletion causes malnutrition.

Vitamins

Vitamins are primarily regulators of biochemical functions. They do not contribute significantly to body structure and are not a direct source of energy. The athlete's need for vitamins is no greater than that of the nonathlete. Vitamin deficiency impairs performance, but vitamin supplementation does not improve it in well-nourished individuals. It is certainly costly. Cooper remarks that "Americans excrete the most expensive urine in the world because it is loaded with so many vitamins!"[5] There is a good deal of fraud in this field. For instance, DMG (N, N-dimethyl glycine) is often publicized as vitamin B_{15} or pangamic acid. The Food and Drug Administration knows of no studies which show it to be a vitamin, and the chemical structure of pangamic acid has never been defined.

Massive doses of the fat soluble vitamins (A, D, E, and K) have been shown to be detrimental to good health. Among the water soluble vitamins, niacin and ascorbic acid (vitamin C) have been demonstrated to be deleterious when taken in excessive quantities. The reason that central European athletes respond favorably to an increased vitamin intake is simply that their diet is normally deficient in certain chemicals.

It is possible, however, that athletes such as jockeys, boxers, and wrestlers who must stay on a low-calorie diet in order to "make weight" or who must train very strenuously for competition may require more vitamins than they can obtain in the normal dietary intake. What all of this seems to add up to is that if a person lives in a rooming house and eats poorly balanced meals or is "making weight" for competition, vitamin-mineral supplementation of food intake may be desirable. A properly balanced diet is the basis of good nutrition. If you want to experiment by taking dietary additives, that is your privilege. It is your money, but you should be careful not to delude yourself by attributing to the additives results that could have been achieved without them.

On the bright side, there is some evidence that new methods of chemical analysis now in the development stage will prove able to identify nutritional deficiences and make corrections in an individual's dietary regimen.

Drugs

During the last few years, the greatest problem in athletics, and in weight training particularly, has been the use of anabolic steroids, the so-called tissue-building drugs. These are synthetic compounds which replicate natural hormones produced by the body, and are believed to promote muscular growth. They are some times prescribed by physicians to treat metabolic problems resulting in reduced ability to assimilate protein, but one survey found that the athletes who served as subjects were taking four to eight times the recommended therapeutic dosage.[6] Steroids may have highly undesirable side effects. Liver damage, endocrine disturbances, testicular atrophy, and impotence in males have been reported to result from their use. Blood pressure may become elevated and the risk of cardiovascular disease is increased. Acne often becomes worse and a tendency to baldness is accelerated.[7] At least one death from liver cancer has been charged to the use of anabolic steroids. Nevertheless, it should be noted that the results of research studies are sometimes conflicting. This appears to be largely due to the number of different drugs that have been used. Apparently, they do cause the body to retain water, which may result in increased weight and body measurements.

At least five athletes, including two weight lifters, were disqualified for life for drug use at the Los Angeles Olympics, and a British journal has charged that 59 Soviet athletes have died in the past 25 years from the excessive use of stimulants, steroids, and other drugs. Suspension for life by the body governing one's sport, by a university or college or, in the case of professional athletes, the team owners or league "czar," and the possibility of early death are heavy penalties to pay for the use of substances whose principal effect is to undermine one's health. With such odds as these, it is difficult to understand how anyone could be so unintelligent as to resort to drugs.

Alcohol and Tobacco

There is no evidence that moderate consumption of alcohol has any deleterious effects on the development of strength and hypertrophy. In fact, claims have been made that small quantities of beer or wine are beneficial to health. Be that as it may, excessive alcohol ingestion adversely affects both heart and skeletal muscle and may be implicated in certain forms of cancer. While there is little direct evidence that the use of tobacco is detrimental to the development of strength, its connection with lung cancer and vascular disease and a decrease in performance at high work loads is well established. This has led the International Federation of Sports Medicine to issue a position paper taking a strong stand against tobacco abuse.[8]

Recent studies demonstrate that cigarette smoking is associated with sleep problems. Difficulties in getting to sleep and sleeping soundly are attributed to the stimulant effects of nicotine, and afford yet another reason for the weight trainer to avoid the use of tobacco.

The use of anabolic steroids has become the number one problem in athletics, particularly in weight training. Can you name at least five physiologically undesirable side effects that may result?

Weight Losing

The traditional prescription for normalizing the body weight for those wishing to reduce is to use low resistance and high repetitions; for those seeking to gain, it is to use high resistance and low repetitions. The fact is, weight training is not very effective in reducing weight unless dietary intake is also regulated. Wilmore *et al.*[9] put subjects of both sexes through a training program consisting of three trips around a ten station circuit and concluded that an average 175 lb. male would lose approximately 1/3 pound of fat per month if he worked out three days a week. This does not mean that he would actually lose any weight. The fat would be replaced by muscle, so that the man might actually weigh more. The effect of the exercise would be to produce a change in body composition rather than in weight.

The basic principle is that the amount of energy expended in exercise must be greater than the amount of energy taken in as food. On the other hand, people who go on a strict diet only may lose muscle tone together with body weight. A combination of increased exercise and decreased food intake appears to be the answer. The addition of running to the training program is often recommended. The diet should be carefully planned to make sure it contains sufficient vitamins and minerals, but there appears to be no particular advantage to either low-carbohydrate or low-fat diets. The caloric intake should be not less than 1,200 per day for females and 1,500 for males. The goal is a loss of two or three pounds per week. A diet as low as 800 calories daily may cause heart damage.

Many individuals who are trying to control their weight do not find such statistics as the number of calories in a doughnut particularly meaningful. For them it may be more significant to reflect that to offset the consumption of one doughnut requires 24 minutes of brisk walking or 13 minutes of jogging. Those who find it easier to think of the effects of food intake in terms of exercise equivalents will find Konishi's *Exercise Equivalents of Food*[10] a helpful guide.

What advice would you give to someone who asks about the best way to lose weight?

Weight Gaining

Progressive resistance exercises are more successful when used as an aid in putting on weight, perhaps in part because the exercise makes the subject hungry and he is encouraged to eat more. Salavantis[11] found that over a period of one semester high school boys on a weight training program gained 7.8 pounds, while those in regular physical education classes gained only 4.6 pounds.

Around 1930 the idea of concentrating on a few heavy exercises for weight gain was introduced. Squats, bent arm pullovers, dead lifts, supine presses, and two-arm presses are examples. These are now accepted procedures among weight trainers. Vern Weaver, Mr. America 1963, used only five exercises when trying to increase his body weight: decline presses, high pull-ups, parallel squats, wide grip chins, and straight-arm pull-downs. He used five or six sets of the same number of repetitions, employing as much weight as possible. Joe Abbenda, Mr. America 1962, spent the first two years of his training performing just three exercises: the squat, the dead lift, and the bench press. These programs are helpful in increasing body weight, but do not by themselves produce attractive physiques. Their proponents insist that the proper way to attain maximum development and shapeliness is to "bulk up, train down."

References

1. Smith, Nathan J. 1982. Nutrition and the Athletes. *American Journal of Sports Medicine* 10:253–55.
2. Spitler, Diana L., *et al.* 1980. Body composition and maximal aerobic capacity of bodybuilders. *Journal of Sports Medicine and Physical Fitness* 20:181–88.
3. Kris-Etherton, P. M. 1985. Nutrition, Exercise and Athletic Performance. *Food & Nutrition News* 57.
4. U.S. FEDERAL TRADE COMMISSION, Advertising and Labeling of Protein Supplements (January 15, 1979), Appendix C, p. 170.
5. Cooper, Donald L. 1972. Drugs and the Athlete. *Journal of the American Medical Association* 221:1007–11.
6. Burkett, Lee N., and Michael T. Falduto. 1984. Steroid Use by Athletes in a Metropolitan Area. *Physician and Sports medicine* 12:69–74.
7. Strauss, Richard H., *et al.* 1983. Side Effects of Anabolic Steroids in Weight-Trained Men. *Physician and Sports-medicine* 12:87–96.
8. International Federation of Sports Medicine (FIMS). Statement on smoking and health. ASCM Sports Medicine Bulletin 15:4.
9. Wilmore, Jack H., *et al.* 1978. Energy cost of circuit weight training. *Medicine and Science in Sports* 10:75–78.
10. Konishi, Frank. 1975. *Exercise Equivalents of Foods.* Carbondale: Southern Illinois University Press.
11. Salavantis, John E. 1972. A comparison of Body Weight Gain of a Group in a Weight Training Program Compared to a Group in a Physical Education Class Without a Weight Training Program. Unpublished Master's Report, Kansas State University.

General References

American College of Sports Medicine. The Use of Anabolic-Androgenic Steroids in Sports, revised 1984. Medicine and Science in Sports and Exercise 19:534–39.

AMA Council on Scientific Affairs. 1987. Vitamin Preparations as Dietary Supplements and as Therapeutic Agents. *Journal of the American Medical Association* 257:1929–36.

Safety Precautions in Weight Training

3

Prior to World War II, weight trainers were largely young men working in their own homes. Since that time, the centers of this activity have become the high schools, colleges, and commercial gymnasia, and women now play a prominent role in its practice. One result is that while injury records are no doubt incomplete, they are much better than they formerly were. A study made in 1979 by the National Electronic Injury Surveillance System of weight trainers of both sexes calculated there were 31,511 injuries, of which one-third were strains or sprains, followed by contusions and abrasions. Of these, 366 cases required hospitalization, 270 of them being fractures.[1] Rather surprisingly, the most frequently injured body parts were the fingers, suggesting some carelessness in loading and unloading the bars.

A study of high school athletes found that the most frequent weight training trauma occurs in the lumbrosacral area, followed by the knee joint.[2] Strains of the long muscles of the back are the predominant soft tissue injury.[3] Incidence of backache and the occurrence of radiological changes in the spine are common.[4]

It is not possible to determine from these reports what lifts or exercises were responsible for these injuries. Most likely many of them were incurred by individuals practicing weight lifting or power lifting rather than weight training. One important factor may be that the weights lifted today are much heavier than was true a generation ago. The handling of maximal or near-maximal weights involves a considerable degree of risks. As lifters more closely approach the stress limits that can be tolerated by the human body, the chances of exceeding these limits increase. When they are exceeded, the results may be disastrous. During the 1984 Olympic competition, a lifter representing the United States was seriously injured while attempting to snatch 286.5 lbs. No weight trainer would attempt to handle this much weight during a training session, but the incidence demonstrates the need for adequate supervision of novice exercisers to ensure that the movements are performed correctly and that the trainee is not overloaded.

This chapter will deal only with the general precautions to be observed. Comments on safety precautions to be observed during specific exercises will be included where appropriate in the descriptions of exercises described in the following chapters.

Causes of Injuries

DuBreuil[5] identifies the five principal causes of injuries in weight training as:

1. Body not strong enough to support the load
2. Body out of proper position to sustain the stress
3. Unevenly developed musculature
4. Limitations in range of motion
5. Failure of the antagonists to relax quickly enough

In a survey of injuries to weight trainers of both genders, what was the most frequently injured part of the body, and what precaution does this suggest?

General Safety Precautions

Medical authorities[6,7] recommend the following safety precautions be observed.

1. Avoid training alone if at all possible.
2. Keep the weight close to the body when lifting.
3. Use correct techniques in all exercises.
4. Do not lift a weight from the floor when you are in a stooping position.
5. Avoid exaggerated "lean back" when pressing a weight overhead.
6. Avoid "hollowing" the lower back when holding a weight overhead.

Examine this drawing. What safety precautions are being violated? What corrections should be made?

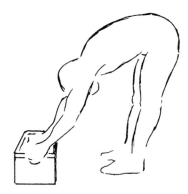

Blackouts

A person pressing a heavy weight has a distinct tendency to hold his or her breath. The weight tends to compress the chest, and a high intrathoracic pressure is produced. There is a sudden rise in blood pressure which prevents the return of the venous blood to the heart. This causes an equally sudden drop in blood pressure, and the lifter may become dizzy and feel faint. This is known to exercise physiologists as the Valsalva phenomenon (Valsalva was a seventeenth-century Italian anatomist) and may be deliberately used by wrestlers in such holds as the bear hug. A lifter will say that he grayed out or blacked out.

A second danger is that the Valsalva maneuver may increase intra-abdominal pressure to such an extent that an inguinal hernia could be produced if there were a preexisting weakness in that area. These considerations suggest that breathing squats may be potentially dangerous to some individuals and are best omitted from the training program.

Compton and associates[8] offer three suggestions to prevent blackouts.

1. Avoid hyperventilation before the lift.
2. Stay in the squatting position as short a time as possible.
3. Raise the weight as rapidly as possible to a position where normal breathing can be resumed.

Precisely because blackouts do occur, many writers on weight training stress detailed instructions in proper breathing. Unfortunately, their advice is frequently contradictory. The most common instruction is to inhale while contracting the muscles and exhale as they are relaxed, but some experts believe the lifter should first take a deep breath and then exhale while lifting. There seems to be an absence of research studies on this.

As in any other form of activity overtraining (i.e., exercising to the point of chronic fatigue) will reduce both performance capacity and the body's ability to resist infection.

What physiological changes occur during the Valsalva phenomenon, and what are the possible dangerous effects to the weight lifter?

Weight Training and Adolescents

The question of whether adolescents should engage in weight training has been debated for the last fifty years. Those opposed argue that the risk of injury is unacceptably high, that prepubertal boys do not make significant gains in strength because of insufficient circulating androgens, and that the stimulus of heavy weights may cause the epiphyses to close earlier so that the individual does not attain his potential height. In particular, students of the problem are concerned about the mechanical effect of the weights on the lumbar region of the spinal column.

In July 1982, the American Academy of Pediatrics issued a policy statement entitled "Weight Training and Weight Lifting: Information for the Pediatrician." The Academy argued that maximal benefits are obtained from weight training by the post-pubertal student, weight lifting should not be practiced by the pre-adolescent, and weight lifting is acceptable for teenagers only if capable supervision is available. Obviously, instructors acting against medical advice do so at their own risk.

Contra Indications

Most men and women will profit from weight training. There are, however, certain conditions in which it is contraindicated. Those suffering from hernia, high blood pressure, fever, infection, recent surgery, or heart disease should avoid it. It is not possible to "sweat out" a cold, and there is a great deal of evidence that vigorous activity during a period of infection serves to spread throughout the body organisms which might otherwise have been sealed off and rendered relatively harmless. The result may be serious, if not fatal. Similarly, trying to hasten the metabolism of alcohol by exercising is useless and may be dangerous.

Hypertension

High blood pressure, particularly prevalent among the super heavyweights, is a matter of concern to physicians. Researchers have recorded dramatic increases in blood pressure in experienced bodybuilders following weight training exercises. A sudden headache after an intensive training session requires immediate medical attention, as it may signal an impending cerebrovascular accident. As one becomes older, the blood vessels become less elastic, increasing the danger.

Warm-up

Most weight trainers warm up with a series of calisthenic exercises, giving particular attention to stretching the back muscles. It has not been proven that warm-up and stretching are of any value in the prevention of injury and some investigators seriously question their worth for this purpose. However, they have the sanction of tradition and there is evidence that sudden bursts of high intensity exercise without prior warm-up result in changes in the electrocardiogram attributable to an inadequate oxygen supply to the heart.

What does research tell us in regard to "sweating out a cold" and exercising to hasten the metabolism of alcohol?

The exerciser should be careful to keep the body warm during the work out, especially when taking rest pauses. The use of a sweatshirt and sweat-pants is highly recommended if the exercise area is not comfortably warm. A temperature of about 68 degrees F. or a little warmer is generally preferred.

Isometric Exercise

Static exercises may be hazardous to individuals with heart problems. It creates a marked rise in arterial pressure and the heart is subjected to an increased oxygen demand, but the increase in blood pumped by the heart is relatively small. Historically, clinical opinion has held that isometric exercise should not be recommended for people of middle age or with coronary artery disease. Recent studies indicate it is probably less dangerous than has been assumed. It may be beneficial under certain circumstances. In each case, safe guidelines should be established on the basis of the individual's history.[9]

References

1. U.S. Consumer Product Safety Commission, Hazard Identification and Analysis, National Electronic Injury Surveillance System, Weight Lifting, Calendar Year 1979. October 25, 1982.
2. Brady, Thomas A., *et al.* 1982. Weight training-related injuries in the high school athlete. *American Journal of Sports Medicine* 10:1–5.
3. Beuker, F. 1970. Weightlifting Injuries and Their Treatment. Federation Halterophile Internationale, Bulletin 167.
4. Aggrawal, N. D., *et al.* 1979. A Study of Changes in the Spine in Weight Lifters and Other Athletes. *British Journal of Sports Medicine* 13:58–61.
5. DuBreuil, Dennis. 1976. Injuries and Their Treatment. *Iron Man* 37:15 *et seq.*
6. Jackson, Frederick E., *et al.* 1974. Weight Lifting Injuries. *Journal of the American College Health Association* 19:187–89.
7. Troup, J. D. G. 1970. The Risk of Weight-Training and Weight-Lifting in Young People. *British Journal of Sports Medicine* 5:27–33.
8. Compton, D., *et al.* 1973. Weight-Lifters' Blackout. *Lancet* 2:1234–37.
9. Fardy, Paul S. 1981. Isometric Exercise and the Cardiovascular System. *Physician and Sportsmedicine* 9:43–56.

Basic Weight Training Program

4

The person without previous weight training experience begins by following a routine designed to produce all-around development. Experience over the years has resulted in the development of a rather standardized set of exercises for this purpose. Most of these derive from a book by Theodor Siebert, published in Germany in 1907. Regardless of whose course one takes or whose book is bought, the recommended basic series will be quite similar to the exercises listed and discussed in the pages that follow.

In all exercises in which the movement starts with the weight at the chest, the trainer brings it to that position by a simplified version of what is known to weight lifters as the *clean*. Start with the feet on line, the knees bent, and the bar close to the shins (fig. 4.1, left). Forcibly extend the knees and pull the bar as nearly straight upward as is possible, taking a short step forward if necessary to bring the bar onto the upper part of the chest (fig. 4.1, right). The weights should be loose enough on the bar so that they will rotate freely as the arms are snapped under the bar for presses or as the bar rises toward the chest in curling. If they are not, the exerciser will develop sore wrists.

Other than a barbell, the only piece of equipment required for the following exercises is a bench. If the lifter builds his own, it should not be over eleven inches wide, of sturdy construction, and with a wide base which will prevent tipping.

Basic Program

Two-Arms Standing Press

The bar is taken to the chest as described, pushed to arms' length overhead, and then lowered to the chest (fig. 4.2). As it passes the head, the weight should move backward a little so that it is in line with the line of gravity of the body. Too far forward or too far backward and control of it will be lost. No spring should be imparted by flexing and straightening the knees (termed a *hitch* by weight trainers), and the exerciser should not lean backward. Most experienced lifters prefer to have the thumbs under the bar and alongside the index fingers while pressing. The press develops the shoulders and the arm extensors: triceps, deltoids, upper part of the trapezius, serratus anterior, and associated muscle groups.

A warning is required here: The medical literature contains reports of a number of cases in which adolescents have sustained fractures of forearm bones while practicing overhead lifts. These resulted when the patients lost control of

Figure 4.1
Modified Barbell Clean. Left: Proper position for lifting a weight to the chest. Note that the feet are in line with the bar, not one foot forward and one back. This subject has his thumb over the bar. Most men prefer to lift it to the chest with the thumb under the bar and make the change before starting the press. Right: The weight is started upward by forceful extension of the knees. The lifter steps forward and under the bar as the weight is snapped onto the top of his chest, and his elbows whip under it. (Photographs by Gene Mozee.)

Figure 4.2
Two-Arms Standing Press. (Photographs by Tony Takash.)

Figure 4.3
Two-Arms High Pull-Up.

the weights so that the weights fell backward, acutely extending the wrists back-wards. Novices should be carefully instructed in the proper technique of such exercises before being allowed to practice them.

High Pull-Up

The bar is held against the front of the thighs, palms in. It is then pulled up to the chin, the elbows raised as high as possible, and lowered to the starting position (fig. 4.3). The high pull-up develops the shoulder and the arm flexors: trapezius, deltoids, biceps, brachialis, brachioradialis, and associated muscle groups.

Two-Arms Curl (Front Curl)

The bar is held against the front of the thighs, palms out. The elbows are kept close to the sides, and the weight is alternately brought up to the chest and low-ered to the starting position (fig.4.4). The tendency to permit the elbows to move backward or to heave the weight up by bending backward at the waist must be avoided. The exercise can be made in strict form by placing the back against the wall or a post. The bar should be lowered slowly and under full control to take advantage of exercising during the eccentric contraction phase of the movement. It is important to fully extend the elbows at the conclusion of this part of the exercise. The two-arms curl develops the arm flexors: biceps, brachialis, bra-chioradialis, and associated muscle groups.

Reverse Curl

This exercise is performed in a manner similar to the previous exercise, with the exception that the palms are turned in instead of out (fig 4.5). It develops much the same muscles as the regular curl, but the exerciser will be able to handle only about two-thirds as much weight due to a change in the mechanical advantage of one of the elbow flexors.

Figure 4.4
Two-Arms Curl. (Photographs by Tony Takash.)

Figure 4.5
Reverse Curl. (Photographs by Tony Takash.)

Some bodybuilders favor special curling bars. These provide vertical sections for gripping so that curls may be performed with the hands in the intermediate as well as in the front and reverse positions. This is especially helpful in developing the brachioradialis.

Half-Squat (Parallel Squat)

The bar is brought up to the chest in the usual manner. The knees are first flexed somewhat and then strongly extended. Simultaneously, the arms are straightened so that the barbell is hurled above the head. It is then carefully lowered to rest on the shoulders behind the head. There is likely to be an uncomfortable pressure against the vertebrae, and the bars are frequently wrapped in the center with towels, foam plastic, or other soft materials or bent so as to remove this pressure.

Figure 4.6
Half-Squat.

The exerciser squats until the thighs are parallel to the floor, keeping the heels on the ground, and then rises, fully straightening the knees (fig. 4.6). The back must be kept as straight as possible, not permitted to round. Studies of power lifters provide a hint for technique in this exercise: The best squatters use the least forward lean of the torso. Students of weight training believe the squat is the fundamental exercise for the development of strength.

Some individuals will find that their quadriceps and hamstrings (semitendinosus and semimembranosus) are so tight that they cannot keep their heels on the floor. This forces them into a deep knee bend, with the consequent danger of falling forward. To obviate this, a two-by-four-inch plank or a thick barbell plate may be placed under the heels, allowing the lifter to shift his or her weight backward. The **deep knee bend** places a little different stress on the quadriceps than does the squat, and some bodybuilders perform both exercises for developmental purposes.

Advanced exercisers sometimes do squats with the barbell held at the collar bones (**front squats**). The back must be kept straight and the head up, or the lifter will lose his balance. The exercise is said to be excellent for the development of the thigh just above the knees, but many experienced individuals dislike it because breathing becomes difficult. Considerably less weight can be handled in front squats than in regular squats.

Back injuries may occur from trying to lift a weight that is too heavy. How can you tell whether you should immediately discontinue your attempt?

Before very long, a lifter will reach the point at which more weight is used for the squats than can be lifted overhead. At that time, a pair of adjustable squat racks or standards becomes invaluable (fig. 4.7). These are set at a height low enough so that the bar will clear the horns when the trainer stands up with the weight on his shoulders. After assuming the erect position, the lifter takes two steps backward, performs the exercises, and then steps forward and replaces the bar, looking first to one side and then to the other to make certain that it is in proper position before bending the knees and stepping out from under it.

Figure 4.7
Vern Weaver, Mr. America 1963, using adjustable squat racks. (Photograph courtesy of York Barbell Company.)

Full squats and full deep knee bends have been condemned by the National Federation of State High School Athletic Associations and the Committee on the Medical Aspects of Sports of the American Medical Association as potentially dangerous to the internal and supporting structures of the knee joint. It is reported, however, that some professional football teams still use the complete movement. It is rare for an individual with damaged knees to attribute them to doing full squats or deep knee bends. However, a large number of exercisers complain of an aching back resulting from permitting the spine to round to the point that the buttocks were the first part of the body to rise. Any attempt to lift a heavy weight should be halted if the hips cannot be kept below the level of the upper body as the legs are extended. While there is little experimental evidence to justify avoiding complete knee flexion, there are theoretical kinesiological reasons for hesitating to assume this position. Until the question has been clarified, it seems safer to avoid full squats.

In any event, heavy squats are not a desirable exercise for individuals working alone. A person may become fatigued and be unable to arise from the squat position. Dumping the weight without hurting oneself may then prove difficult.

In **"breathing squats"** the lifter places the weight on the shoulders, takes three to six deep breaths, holds the last one, and does a single rapid squat, bouncing up from the deep position, and repeats this procedure for as many repetitions as desired. There are two serious objections to this procedure: In the first place, bouncing squats are considered to be a cause of knee injuries; in the second place, holding the breath while squatting may induce the **Valsalva maneuver,** which is also undesirable (see p. 19).

Squatting movements develop the knee extensors: quadriceps femoris (rectus femoris, vastus lateralis, vastus intermedius, and vastus medialis).

Figure 4.8
Heel Raises. (Photographs by Tony Takash.)

Heel Raises

Following completion of the squats, the lifter retains the weight on the shoulders and raises the heels as high off the ground as possible (fig. 4.8). The lifter then returns to the starting position. To exercise the involved muscles from several angles, one-third of the repetitions are done with the toes turned out as far as possible, one-third with the toes pointed forward, and one-third with the toes turned in. To increase the resistance, the exerciser may place the toes on the board or plates mentioned, thus increasing the range through which the calf muscles must contract. A popular alternative is to perform the exercise while seated on the bench with the weight resting on the tops of the knees. Most individuals find it necessary to place some sort of padding under the bar. A more advanced approach is to walk up and down a flight of stairs, stepping flat-footed on each tread and rising up on the toes to step onto the next one. Any way it is done, this exercise develops the foot extensors: gastrocnemius, soleus, and associated muscle groups.

Bent-Arm Pull-Over

The exerciser lies supine on the bench, the head at one end, knees bent so that the feet are on the bench, and the entire back in contact with it. Some sway-backed individuals may not be able to achieve this. The weight is held at the chest with the elbows bent. Keeping the elbows in this position, the arms pivot at the shoulders so that the weight is swung past the head, just brushing the hair, and lowered as far as possible without causing the back to lose contact with the bench. No arching of the back is permitted at any stage of the exercise (fig. 4.9). The weight is then returned to the starting position. The elbows must be kept in—not permitted to swing out to the sides. The exercise may also be done with the reverse grip.

Pull-overs are sometimes performed with the elbows straight instead of bent, in which case considerably less weight is used. This method is not recommended since sooner or later the exerciser will use too much poundage and suffer deltoid strain or an overstretch of the elbow joint capsule. If no bench is available, the

Figure 4.9
Bent-Arm Pull-Overs.

exercise can be performed on the floor, but with reduced effect. It develops the upper chest and back: deltoids, pectoralis, latisimus dorsi, teres major, and associated muscle groups.

Straight-Legged Dead Lift (Derrick Lift)

Bend over at the waist and pick the bar up with the alternate grip—that is, one hand facing in and one facing out. This reduces the likelihood that a heavy weight will pull the fingers open as the gripping muscles tire. The exerciser rises to the erect position and contracts the muscles of the upper back as though trying to pull the shoulder blades together. The lifter then bends over again, lowering the weight to not less than two inches from the floor (fig. 4.10). Some experienced trainers stand on a platform and lower the weight until the bar is at ankle level. It is extremely inadvisable for the novice to try this. When the body is fully flexed, the strain is borne by the ligaments of the back, with little or no assistance from the muscles. Direct injury may result, or the ligaments may be stretched and predisposed to further trauma. Because of the weight there is a tendency for the heels to rise off the ground. This must be resisted, or the lifter may end up by falling forward. Blocks may be utilized between the plates and the floor so that the lifter's spine is never full flexed.

The important role that strong abdominal muscles play in counteracting the development of compression fractures and bending lesions of the spine in such exercises is not always appreciated. Well developed abdominals may be a major factor in preventing the onset of low back pain as a result of dead lifting. This suggests the desirability of including bent knee sit ups and body curls in one's program. The difficulty of these exercises can be increased by using weights to provide greater resistance or by performing the exercises on an inclined board.

At this point a word of explanation is required. The straight-legged dead lift is an exercise for the muscles of the back and of the back of the thighs. When lifters talk about dead lifting, they refer to a movement in which they bend the knees and lift the weight by contracting the quadriceps. The training routine for this may include the **Hack lift,** which is a squat with the weight held behind the body, as in figure 4.6, instead of placed on the shoulders, and the straddle lift **(Jefferson and Kennedy lift)** in which the lifter straddles a barbell, one foot forward and one back, and lifts it by straightening the knees. These are actually variations of the squat and would have been included under the discussion of that

Figure 4.10
Straight-Legged Dead Lift.

exercise if it had not been necessary to clarify the fact that there are two distinct styles of dead lifting. The same precautions should be observed for the Hack lift and the straddle lift as with squatting—that is, the squat should be made to only the parallel position. The straight-legged dead lift develops the extensors of the back and hip: erector spinae, gluteus maximus, semitendinosus, semimembranosus, and related muscle groups. The Hack and straddle lifts develop primarily the quadriceps.

Why is it recommended in the straight-legged dead lift that the bar be picked up with the alternate grip (i.e., one hand facing in and one hand facing out)?

The **sumo style of dead lifting** shown in figure 4.11 illustrates how a standard lift may be modified to be more specific to a given activity, how variety may be introduced into a training program, and how variations in technique may introduce different muscle stresses. In this method, the leg adductors are affected more directly than in the standard technique. Whether practice of this position would result in more knee injuries remains an open question.

A variation of the straight-legged dead lift is the **"good morning exercise"** in which the barbell is placed on the shoulders in back of the neck and the exerciser first bends forward and then to each side. Only light weights should be used, and no attempt should be made to fully flex the trunk.

Another excellent exercise for developing the back muscles is the so-called **swan exercise** in which a man lies face downward and then extends his torso. This is shown in figure 6.1. In advanced training, a weight may be held behind the head. The main difficulty is finding some way to securely anchor the feet. It should not be practiced by those with back problems.

Figure 4.11
Hollis L. Evett demonstrating the start and finish of sumo style of dead lifting. (Photo courtesy of Ultimate Equipment.)

Bench Press (Supine Press)

The practice of bench presses came into general use in the early 1930s, and is very popular today largely due to the emphasis placed on them by football linemen and weight throwers. The exerciser lies on his back on a bench with the weight at his chest. The bar is pushed to arm's length and then lowered to the chest (fig. 4.12). It must come to a rest so that it is not bounced up off the chest.

Certain precautions should be taken during this exercise. If the weight gets off to one side, it may cause the bench to tip. For this reason the feet should be placed on the floor in a good position to resist any tendency of the bench to tip. The head should be at the end of the bench so that the weight can be dropped to the floor behind it if it tends to get away from the lifter.

This is probably the most popular and at the same time the most dangerous of the weight training exercises. Exercisers training alone should avoid the bench press. Lifters who have become fatigued have dropped the weight on their chests,

Figure 4.12
Bench Press. Note that the thumbs are under the bar.

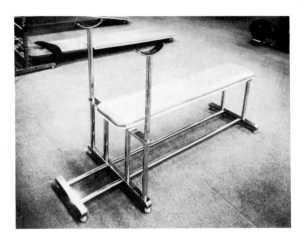

Figure 4.13
Supine Bench with Integral Standards. (Photograph courtesy of Paramount Gymnasium Equipment Corp.)

throats, or faces, sometimes with fatal results. At least one female lifter has been killed in this manner. It should not be practiced unless there is a partner available to assist in the event the lifter gets into trouble.

If the supine press is done on the floor, the use of extra large plates will enable the lifter to roll the weight over his head to the starting position and will protect him if his arms cannot support the weight. If the exercise is performed on a bench, it is strongly recommended that the barbell be placed on some form of supports from which it can be lifted to start the exercise and to which it can be returned upon completion of the presses. Some of the commercially built benches have standards as an integral part of the bench (fig. 4.13), which is both a convenience and a safeguard.

The position of the hands may be varied from close together to wide apart in order to work the muscles from different angles. The farther apart the hands, the greater the stress on the pectorals; the closer the hands, the greater the stress on the triceps. To a lesser degree, the spacing of the hands affects the deltoids. There have been a number of reports of shoulder and pectoral injuries resulting from the practice of extremely wide hand spacing. The powerlifting rules allow 32 in. spacing, but this may be excessive. Perhaps 24 to 28 in. should be the maximum.

The bench press develops the extensors of the arms, the shoulders, and the chest: triceps, deltoids, and pectoralis major, together with associated muscle groups. The enormous weights that can be handled in this exercise sometimes result in tears of the pectoralis major.

The most dangerous, as well as probably the most popular, weight training exercise is the bench press. Which of the precautions is the most important?

Press Off the Back of the Neck (POBN)

The barbell is placed on the shoulders behind the neck, as for the squat. The exercise may be done standing, which enables you to use a little more weight, but it is usual for the lifter to straddle the bench and sit down. The weight is pressed to arms' length overhead and then lowered to the shoulders behind the neck (fig. 4.14). The head must be kept slightly forward to avoid being hit by the bar as it goes up and down. It is essential that the bar not be dropped on the vertebrae of the neck during the lowering phase of the movement. Care must also be taken to see that the weight does not get too far behind the trainer as he or she may seriously damage the arms and shoulders in attempting to control it. Many experienced weight trainers consider this the basic exercise for the shoulders.

A variation of this exercise is to alternately lower the bar to the chest and to the shoulders behind the head, thus combining the two exercises into one. The press behind the neck develops the arm extensors and the shoulders: triceps, deltoids, trapezius, and associated muscle groups.

Rowing Motion

The lifter picks the weight up with the palms turned in, bends over at the waist, flattening the back as much as possible and keeping the knees slightly bent, and lets the arms hang down. The weight is then pulled up to the chest, the elbows are allowed to go out so that they are more or less in line with the shoulders, and then the weight is lowered again (fig. 4.15). An effective variation is to pick up the weight with the palms turned outward and bring it to the waist, keeping the elbows as close to the sides as possible. A second variation is to load one end of a barbell, place the other in a corner, straddle the bar, and perform rowing motions in this fashion. Bars are available commercially whch are hinged at the floor end. This keeps the base of the apparatus from moving around and damaging the woodwork.

These exercises develop the arm flexors and the back muscles: biceps, radialis, brachioradialis, deltoids, rhomboids, latissimus dorsi, teres major, and associated muscle groups. The first variation has more effect on the latissimus dorsi than do the other two techniques.

Figure 4.14
Seated Press Off the Back of the Neck.

Figure 4.15
Rowing Motion to the Chest. (Photographs by Tony Takash.)

Some instructors contend that this position should never be assumed because the long lever and the weight of the trunk, head, arms, and resistance place a great strain on the lower back muscles. While I have never heard of anyone being injured while performing rowing motions, the position might be hazardous for those with lower back problems. It is safer if the exercise is performed with the head resting on some sort of a support, which will remove any possibility of back strain.

Wrestler's Bridge

The exercise starts in the supine position on the floor with knees bent. Rock up onto the crown of the head, lifting the buttocks and shoulders from the floor. Individuals not accustomed to this exercise will find it rather strenuous and are likely to incur a very sore neck if they go at it too vigorously at first. After a period of training without a weight, the exerciser may take a barbell at the chest, thrust it to arm's length as he or she rocks up on the head, and lower it again to the chest when returning to the starting position (fig. 4.16). The exerciser should conclude by assuming the prone position, rolling up on to the crown of the head,

Figure 4.16
Wrestler's Bridge. (Photographs by Gene O'Connell.)

and vigorously exercising the neck in this position. A foam rubber pad or some other sort of protection will be needed to keep the scalp from hurting during bridges. Advanced exercisers may do bent-arm pull-overs in this position, but this should not be attempted by beginners.

It is difficult to introduce much in the way of variation in neck exercises unless one buys a head strap from which weights can be suspended, or a helmet on which they can be loaded or has a training partner with whom he can perform "bulling" and the other exercises employed by wrestlers. One alternative to the towel exercises frequently used when a partner is available is to hang an inner tube from a hook, place the head inside, and flex the neck muscles in every possible direction against the elastic resistance provided by the tube. Another is a cable run from a head strap over a pulley mounted on the wall and then to a holder for weights.

The principal superficial muscle visibly affected by neck exercises is the sternocleidomastoid. Although a large number of associated muscle groups are also affected, they are difficult to differentiate in the living subject.

Many experienced exercisers would probably add one or more of the following movements to the foregoing program. It would be just as well not to include them at the beginning of training, but if desired, they could be employed after one becomes somewhat accustomed to the exertion of barbell training.

Wrist Curls

The exerciser fits with forearms on thighs (fig. 4.17) or on a table. If preferred, kneel down and use the flat bench in place of a table. Hold a barbell in the hands, palms up. The wrists are alternately extended and flexed through the full range of movement. This exercise may also be performed with the palms down, in which case it is known as the **reverse wrist curl.**

The wrist curl develops the flexors of the forearm: flexor carpi radialis, flexor carpi ulnaris, and associated muscle groups. The reverse wrist curl develops the extensors of the forearm: extensor carpi radialis, extensor carpi ulnaris, and associated muscle groups.

An alternate exercise is the **wrist roller.** A cord is run through a hole drilled through the middle of a short piece of wood or pipe. Weights are suspended from the cord. The exerciser holds the bar in front with both hands and rotates it so

Figure 4.17
Wrist Curls.

Figure 4.18
Shoulder Shrug. (Photographs by Gene Mozee.)

that the cord wraps around the bar. Such a unit may be easily mounted on a wall if desired. In use, a set in which the bar is revolved in one direction is followed by a set in which it is rotated in the other.

The forearms, like the calves, are usually very difficult to develop. To save possible disappointment, it should be pointed out that while the correlation between the girth of the forearm and the strength of the hand grip is moderately high, development of a strong grip requires movements specifically designed to exercise the finger and thumb flexors in addition to forearm training. These may include grasping a heavy barbell plate and passing it from one hand to the other, carrying a sack of sand or some similar material by one hand, squeezing a sponge rubber ball, taking a sheet of newspaper by one corner and crumpling it up into a tight ball in one hand, or using any of the numerous spring resistance devices found on the market.

Shoulder Shrug

Stand in front of the barbell, squat, grasp the bar with the hands, and stand erect. Then contract the shrugging muscles, raise the shoulders as high as possible as though trying to touch the deltoids to the ears (fig. 4.18). Most persons seem to prefer to work with the palms turned out. The exercise may also be done with the weight held in front, in which case the palms are usually turned in. In either case, the shoulder elevators are developed: trapezius, levator scapulae, rhomboid, and associated muscle groups.

Triceps Extension (French Press; Triceps Press)

The exerciser stands or sits with the barbell overhead at arm's length as though completing a press. The arms must be close to the ears. The upper arms are kept in this position while the elbows are flexed so that the bar comes down in back of the head. The elbows must be kept perpendicular while the bar is being raised (fig. 4.19). The exerciser will find that there is a decided tendency for them to move outward if the weight is a little on the heavy side. While this is an excellent exercise, it has the reputation of producing sore elbows, and some individuals may find it impossible to use.

Figure 4.19
Triceps Extension. (Photographs by Gene Mozee.)

A variation of this exercise can be done by lying supine on a bench, pressing the weight to arm's length, and then lowering and raising it as described.

Additional Exercises

Individuals with a large abdomen may wish to add bent knee sit-ups, leg raises, and vee-ups to this program in order to directly exercise their abdominal muscles. The difficulty of the first two movements may be increased by use of an inclined board.

Weights and Repetitions

As was explained in chapter 1, the results of a program of progressive resistance exercise seem to depend upon three variables: (1) the amount of stress placed on the muscles, (2) the duration of the exercise periods, and (3) the frequency of the exercise periods. The possible combinations of these three factors and the range of human differences in response to each are so great that researchers have hardly scratched the surface of their possible combinations. We do not even know whether programs designed to produce hypertrophy should differ from those designed to produce strength and, if so, in what ways. As a result of these factors, the following suggestions are empirical rather than scientific.

The novice should start with weights that can be handled with comparative ease. Colfer[1] suggests the following as estimated starting loads:

Exercise	Estimated Starting Weight
1. Bench Press	66-2/3% of Bodyweight (BW)
2. Parallel Squat	66-2/3% of BW
3. Bent Over Rowing	50% of BW
4. Upright Rowing	33-1/3% of BW
5. Shoulder Shrug	50% of BW
6. Bent Knee Dead Lift	75% of BW
7. Power Clean	50% of BW
8. Bent-Arm Pull-Over	25% of BW

9. Seated Press	33-1/3% of BW
10. Press Behind Neck	25% of BW
11. Two-Arm Curl	33-1/3% of BW

From George R. Colfer, "Power Training for Football" in *Athletic Journal*, 59:8, 1978. Copyright © 1978 Athletic Journal Publishing Company, Evanston, IL.

It will usually be observed that after the first two or three weeks, the beginner is able to handle considerably more weight, especially in such exercises as the bench press. This does not mean that strength has greatly increased in that short period. It results from the fact that the exerciser has learned how to balance the weight, how to relax antagonistic muscles, and otherwise how to improve coordination. At that time, the amounts of weight employed in the various exercises will need to be adjusted upward. Thereafter, the exerciser should be able to remain on a schedule for changes in weights and repetitions.

The general rule is to begin with five or six repetitions of each exercise for the arms and ten or twelve for the back and legs. Work out three days a week: Monday, Wednesday, and Friday. It should be anticipated that with proper warm-up, rest pauses, and the like, the exercise period will approximate two hours. Each Monday add one repetition to the arm exercises and two to the back and leg exercises. After a week of ten or twelve repetitions for the arms and twenty or twenty-four for the back and legs, increase the weights for the former by five pounds and for the latter by ten pounds, and return to the original five/six and ten/twelve repetitions. There is, of course, an end point to any progression. Sooner or later there will come a time at which the increment must be smaller than suggested. Eventually it may be measured in ounces.

After the first two or three weeks, the novice weight lifter may find that considerably heavier weights can be handled. What are the principal reasons for the improvement?

The foregoing method is known as the **double progressive system,** since both the weights and the number of repetitions are increased at regular intervals. The older **single progressive system** consisted of keeping the repetitions at a given number but adding weight as frequently as possible. It is seldom seen today except among competitive lifters. Less popular now than some years ago is the **"1001 Exercises"** system. This assumes that the best way to develop muscles is to exercise them in a large number of different ways so that every fiber is stressed. The training program may be changed almost weekly in order to gain new approaches. Such a schedule would seem consistent with the Soviet idea that different stimuli must be presented to a muscle if it is to attain maximal development. But for some reason it does not seem to work out as well as one would expect. Generally speaking, greater development seems to result from more concentrated methods, but this system may have some advantages for those seeking extreme definition of muscle.

Program Evaluation

To a large extent, any program, basic or advanced, can be evaluated by the question, "How do you feel the next morning?" If you are unable to sleep, wake up exhausted, and have to drag yourself out of bed and through the day, you are probably overtraining. All too often the beginner finds his measurements shrinking and his strength decreasing. In desperation he drives himself to still greater exertion. This is precisely the wrong thing to do. A Mr. America may have to train every day if he is to keep in top competitive condition, but it is during the rest periods that his muscles build up. Proper rest is just as important as is proper exercise. The forty-year-old may find that two workouts a week suit him best. Some experienced trainers recommend that every six weeks of hard training be followed by one week away from the weights. When training is resumed, the exercise program is changed. If nothing else, this breaks up the monotony, and one goes back to workouts rested and with renewed enthusiasm.

Under the best of conditions there will be periods when even the experienced weight trainer will not feel up to undertaking the usual program. At such times the intensity of training may be lessened by doing one less set of each exercise or fewer repetitions in each set. It is probably important to maintain the frequency of workouts even though the lifter may have to reduce the intensity in order to do it.

From time to time the reader will encounter suggestions that the intensity of one's workouts be based on the state of the exerciser's biorhythms. However, the idea of biorhythms in the popular sense seems to be without merit and no attention need be paid to these suggestions.[2]

References

1. Colfer, George R. 1978. Power Training for Football. *Athletic Journal* 59:8 *et seq.*
2. Rasch, Philip J. 1980. Biorhythms— Claims and Evaluations. *American Corrective Therapy Journal* 34:15–18.

Weight Training for Women

5

Some time ago, the President's Council on Physical Fitness and Sports complained that most American women lack the necessary strength in their arms, shoulders, and trunk to perform the ordinary tasks required in daily living. One outcome was that many YWCAs installed weight training courses specifically designed to strengthen the upper torsos and arms of women seeking non-traditional jobs. Lack of strength frequently imposes limitations on performance even in women athletes. While there is no question that weight training is the quickest way to develop strength, many women have been afraid that it would increase muscular bulk, giving them a masculine appearance. These fears are groundless. All of the women who climbed Annapura I in 1978 had included weight training in their conditioning programs, as do athletes Linda Webber-Rettie while preparing for long distance yacht races, tennis player Pam Shriver (fig. 5.1), and synchronized swimmers Tracie Ruiz and Candy Costie, winners of the 1984 Olympics gold medal. Professional entertainers, whose personal appearance is a most important asset, also often follow weight training programs.

Perhaps the major innovation in women athletes' training has been the increased emphasis on progressive resistance exercise. Swimming coaches generally agree that the sensational showing made by the East German girls in the Montreal Olympics may be attributed largely to the fact that they spent 25 percent of their training time in the use of weights. According to O'Shea and Wegner,[1] European women have achieved their preeminence in weight throwing events precisely because their weight training program is identical with that of male throwers.

Actually, there are theoretical reasons for suggesting that physiologically women may be better suited to certain athletic events than are men. The quality of female muscle, i.e., contractile properties and ability to exert force, is the same as male muscle. It follows that in this respect, the female has the same potential for strength development as does the male of comparable size and that there are no basic differences between weight training programs for men and for women. The female does not, however, have the same capacity for developing body size and muscular bulk, because the secretion of the male hormone testosterone is considerably higher in the normal man than in the normal woman. It has been estimated that men daily secrete 30–200 micrograms of testosterone, whereas women secrete 5–20 micrograms. Further, exercise is said to have a greater effect on the endocrine secretions of men than of women. As a result, the average woman's strength is about two-thirds that of the average man. If, however, adjustment is made for women's smaller body size, the difference is reduced to about 20 percent.

Figure 5.1
Tennis star Pam Shriver making an "all out" effort on a Nautilus exercise machine during training designed to rehabilitate her right shoulder following an injury resulting from her hand serve. (Photo courtesy of Tennis Magazine. Copyright © 1980.)

The fear of developing bulky musculature has deterred many women from undertaking weight training programs. What is the physiological evidence regarding this concern?

Another reason for the lower strength-weight ratio in women as compared with men of equal weight is their smaller percentage of muscle in relation to their considerably larger amount of adipose tissue. Young women average 27 percent of their body weight as fat, compared with 12 percent for men. Probably much of this difference is due to the women's lesser activity. The only morphological characteristic common to all outstanding athletes, male and female alike, is the low ratio of body fat and the high percentage of lean body mass. Olga Korbut, for instance, is said to have had only 1.5 percent body fat when in strict training.

Alterations in body composition as the result of a high resistance weight training program are nearly identical for both men and women—that is, there is an increase in lean body weight and a decrease in total body fat, with relatively little change in total body weight. In a study of college women MacIntyre[2] found that exercising as little as one-half an hour three times a week for seven weeks resulted in a significant reduction in fat and an increase in muscle. Other investigators have reported similar findings.

While weight training significantly improves the body composition, it does not appear to be an effective method of reducing body weight. Most studies agree that several weeks of weight training will produce little change in body weight. There is a large body of evidence to show that the difference between girls of normal weight and those of overweight is largely a matter of activity rather than of diet. In one study, normal-weight high school girls were shown to have an average intake of 2,706 calories daily, while their obese school mates averaged only 1,965 calories. While diet must be controlled, the daily difference in calorie use between an active and a sedentary woman can easily amount to 500 calories, which would consume a pound of fat in a week. Perhaps the most effective approach is to include running in the training program. However, some women have unusually low basal metabolic rates and find it extremely difficult to lose weight even on a regimen of this kind. This is particularly true of those who have been dieting for an extended period.

It was shown in one study that obese high school girls consumed fewer calories than did girls of normal weight. Can you account for this finding? How do you suggest that these obese students try to lose weight?

Exercise Programs

There is no need to devise special exercise schedules for females. The same programs are equally effective for both men and women. Wilmore,[3] for instance, successfully trained a coeducational class of college students on a program consisting of half-squats or leg presses, toe raises, two-hand curls, standing presses, bench presses, bent-arm pull-overs, bent rowing motions, and side bends. Price,[4] using women subjects only, employed a routine consisting of triceps extension, parallel squats, supine bench press, bent-knee dead lift, two-hands curl, side bend, latissimus pull-downs, and abdominal curls. The emphasis of the program, however, may be different. It seems to be generally agreed that American women athletes usually lack upper body strength.

Athletes will, of course, have the advantage of being guided by their coaches. For instance, the coaches of Soviet women weight throwers have rejected the use of standard weight training exercises on the grounds that they are not sufficiently similar to the movements in these field events. There is insufficient space here to describe their programs, but those interested in the thinking of our major competitor will find their programs set forth in an article by Sinitskiy.[5] According to O'Shea and Wegner, for the past decade, European and Russian women have dominated international competition in the discus, shot put, and javelin because of their power weight training.

Perhaps as a result, the use of weight training in women athletes is steadily increasing in the United States. The following program for women volleyball players is followed at UCLA:

Leg extension
Leg press
Heel raises
Lunges
Pull-overs
Pull-downs
Double chest press
Shoulder raises
Triceps extension
Straight-arm pull
Good mornings

Table 5.1.   Most Common Feminine Figure Faults and Appropriate Exercises

Fault	Exercise
Conspicuous collar bones and/or undersized bust	Bent-arm pull-overs; flying exercise; bench press with dumbbells
Large abdomen	Bent-knee sit-ups; vee-ups; all forms of side bends and twists
Flabby thighs	Squats; leg press; front, side, and back leg raises; lunges and stair climbing with barbell on shoulders; leg flexion and extension with iron boot
Underdeveloped calves	Heel raises; walking on the toes with barbell on shoulders

During the competitive season these exercises are practiced twice a week. Two sets are completed, the first for 12 repetitions and the second for 8.[6]

The late George Bruce, who produced a large number of beauty contest winners, was probably the first to introduce strenuous weight training into their developmental programs. Amedee Chabot, twice Miss USA, was placed on the following program:

Warm up with dumbbells, 2 x 8
Sit ups, 3 x 15
Dumbbell swing, 3 x 10
Toe touches, 3 x 8
Dead lift, 3 x 8
Bench press, 3 x 8
Leg press, 3 x 8
Dumbbell squat, 3 x 8
Dumbbell lunge, 3 x 8

Any specific program and the poundages and repetitions used must, of course, be designed to suit the needs of the individual. One study[7] has shown that girls who systematically practice the bench press may increase their strength by 3.3 to 4.3 percent per week. Some suggestions for improving the most common figure faults are given in table 5.1.

The weight training programs followed by international level feminine athletes are quite strenuous. For example, rower Joan Lind (fig. 5.2) employs the following off-season training routine:

Slant board leg raises, 2 x 25
Latissimus machine rowing, 4 x 10 with 110–150 lbs., depending on how much the back is used
Bench press, 3 x 10, 100–110 lbs.
Upright rowing, 4 x 10, 70 lbs.
Leg curls, 3 x 10, 50–60 lbs.
Leg extensions, 3 x 10, 100–110 lbs.

Figure 5.2

Joan Lind, a Magna Cum Laude graduate of California State University, Long Beach and America's premier oarswoman. Since the most severe stress in athletics is found in rowing, Ms. Lind surely presents the relatively low ratio of body fat and the high percentage of lean body mass characteristic of athletes. It is evident that this in no way detracts from the femininity of her appearance. Lind won the single sculls silver medal at the Montreal Olympics in 1976, finishing less than a second behind the winner, and a silver medal in the quadruple sculls in the 1984 Olympics. (Photo by Anna Rivera, courtesy of Dr. A. K. Thomas.)

Leg presses, 4 x 10 with 290, 335, 360, and 385 lbs.
Chins, 3 x 5
Bent-knee abdominal curls, 4 x 50
Parallel bar dips, 2 x 5

Some Physiological Considerations

Various studies have indicated that some women suffer more frequent dislocations of the patella and more joint sprains than do men. In part, at least, this may be due to their weaker musculature. Weight training appears to be the most rational approach to the prevention of such injuries, but the use of anabolic steroids for the purpose of stimulating muscular development is potentially as dangerous for women as it is for men. The American College of Sports Medicine's position paper on this subject lists masculinzation, disruption of the normal growth pattern, voice changes, acne, hirsutism, enlargement of the clitoris, disturbances of the menstrual cycle, and possible upset of the reproduction function as among the undesired side effects of their use. Use of drugs by women weight trainers has been charged with the responsibility for the flat-chested appearance so many of them present. The College urges that anyone involved in the care of female athletes "should exercise all persuasions available to prevent the use of anabolic steroids by female athletes."[8] It would be hard to put the case more strongly.

It has been estimated that about 15 percent of American women require regular medicinal iron supplementation. In some instances, use of an iron supplement may prove helpful in improving performance. This is a matter to be discussed with a competent sports physician should one believe that its use might be indicated. The limited research evidence available suggests only that heavy training has no consistent and predictable effects and that, in general, women athletes are similar to nonathletes so far as iron status is concerned.

Recently, some promoters of physique contests have begun staging shows in which the female contestants train down to an extremely lean state to better display muscular definition. Participants in such exhibitions should be aware that a minimum of 22 percent body fat is believed to be necessary for stable reproductive ability and maintenance of normal menstrual cycles in women aged 16 and over. Several studies have shown that in ballet dancers and runners, vigorous physical exercise, alone or in conjunction with reductions of body fat below this "critical minimum body weight" may result in amenorrhea.[9] No studies of female weight trainers in this connection have been found in the literature. Like the question of iron supplementation, if there is cause for concern, a competent sports physician should be consulted.

Recent studies[10] indicate that maximal exercise performance is unaffected by the phase of the menstrual cycle, although its effect on endurance requires further investigation.

Figure Contouring

Quantifying goals to be pursued in figure contouring is almost impossible. If the anthropometry of male physique winners is unreliable (see Chapter 8), that of women beauty winners is almost non-existent. As a result women do not have access to the detailed standards which are available to men. The chest measurement is taken just below the breasts. The waist and calf are taped in the same way as for men. The hips are measured around the largest part, where they are the broadest and the buttocks are the deepest. Beauty contest judges show a preference for figures in which the bust and hip measurements are the same and the waist is approximately 12 inches smaller than either one. Some say the calf should be the same girth as the knee. There appears to be general agreement that most untrained American women tend to have oversized waists and thighs and underdeveloped calves.

The average body fat for men is 12 percent. In the belief that less is better, some women athletes try to emulate this figure. Why is this not advised?

Anthropometrist David Willoughby gave the measurements shown in table 5.2 as representing the average American woman. For comparative purposes, the average measurements of the Miss Americas from 1959–1979 are shown in the same table. These are very incomplete and their accuracy cannot be determined. Comparative data on female bodybuilders is all but nonexistent. It is unfortunate that the promoters of these contests have done such a miserable job of collecting anthropometric measurements, but the data that are available give at least a general idea of the contemporary standards of ideal proportions.

Table 5.2. Anthropometry of American Women

Measurement	Average American Woman	Average of 1959–1979 Miss Americas
Height	64''	66.7''
Neck	12.50''	
Chest	33.4''	
Bust	35''	35.6''
Biceps	10.8''	
Forearm	9.5''	
Waist	26.4''	23.4''
Hips	37.4''	35.55''
Thigh	21.6''	
Knee	14.2''	
Calf	13.6''	
Ankle	8.4''	
Weight	124 lbs.	119.1 lbs.

References

1. John P. O'Shea, and Julie Wegner. June 1981. Power Weight Training and the Female Athlete. *Physician and Sportsmedicine* 9:107–20.
2. Christina MacIntyre. 1967. Effect of a Weight Training Program on Body Contours of Young Women 18–22. Unpublished Master's Thesis. University of California at Los Angeles.
3. Jack H. Wilmore. 1974. Alterations in strength, body composition and anthropometric measurements consequent to a 10-weeks weight training program. *Medicine and Science in Sports* 6:133–38.
4. Sandra Price. 1974. The Effects of Weight Training on Strength, Endurance, Girth, and Body Composition in College Women. Unpublished Master's Thesis. Brigham Young University.
5. Z. Sinitskiy. 1974. Barbell Exercises for Women Throwers. *Yessis Review of Soviet Physical Education and Sports* 9:22–27.
6. Gail Weldon. December 1980. Conditioning Program for Women's Volleyball at UCLA. *National Strength Coaches Association Journal* 21:30–31.
7. Wayne L. Westcott. November-December 1979. Female Response to Weight Training, *Journal of Physical Education* 77:31–33.
8. American College of Sports Medicine. 1984. Position Statement on the Use and Abuse of Anabolic-Androgenic Steroids in Sports. Revised 1984. *Medicine and Science in Sports and Exercise* 19:534–539.
9. Rose E. Frisch, *et al.* July 3, 1980. Delayed Menarche and Amenorrhea in Ballet Dancers. *New England Journal of Medicine* 303:17–19.
10. Mary L. Dombovy, *et al.* 1987. Exercise performance and ventilatory response in the menstrual cycle. *Medicine and Science in Sports and Exercise* 19:111–17.

General Reference

Cureton, K. J., *et al.* 1988. Muscle
hypertrophy in men and women. Medicine
and Science in Sports and Exercise
20:338–344.

Advanced Training Methods

6

One factor which stands out in all studies of progressive resistance exercise is the great individual differences in response to training programs. This makes it impossible to specify a standard program which will be equally suitable for everyone. The exercises, weights, and repetitions suggested in the previous chapter are just that—suggestions. The conclusion would seem to be that any schedule is more or less experimental and must be carefully observed to determine whether it is producing the desired results. Even when the results are satisfactory, it must be anticipated that sooner or later an exerciser will reach a point at which progress no longer seems as fast as desired. This is an indication that the time has come to switch to advanced training methods. Two different approaches are possible: changes in the system of training and in the use of apparatus. These will be discussed in that order. The reader may wonder why, if there are superior systems, he or she should not start with them instead of wasting time on a basic program. All advanced training methods depend upon one basic principle: increasing the amount of stress placed upon the body within the given training period. The beginning weight trainer is no more ready for these levels of work than is a college wrestler prepared for competition on the first day of team workouts. Only rarely should one consider advanced training methods until completion of six months or more on the basic program.

Systems of Training

Chapter 4 presented the single progressive and double progressive systems. There are a number of others, the most popular of which are presented below. It must be said, however, that there is an increasing amount of research evidence, which indicates that there is no significant difference in the end results provided the body is pushed to the same level of effort under each system.

Light and Heavy System

The trainer starts out with a weight considerably lighter than maximal, does a few (perhaps three) repetitions, stops, adds more weight (perhaps five pounds), and performs a few more repetitions, continuing this procedure as long as possible. Toward the end of such a series, the amount of weight added may be decreased to the point that it consists of no more than a couple of iron washers, and the number of repetitions may be decreased from three to two, and finally to one.

This was the method followed by the Egyptians during the years that they were the world's best weight lifters and is still advocated today by many men whose main interest is in the development of strength.

Heavy and Light System

This procedure has been popularized by the lifters at York, Pennsylvania. The individual starts off with the maximum weight that can be handled for a given number of repetitions, completes these, takes off some weight, and again repeats a maximal number of repetitions, repeating this procedure as long as can be continued. The basic principle is to keep the muscle working against near-maximal resistance even though fatigue is reducing its capacity for performance. There is some evidence that this method of training is more effective than is the light and heavy system. This technique is very popular in rehabilitation work, where it is often referred to as the Zinovieff or the Oxford technique. Weight trainers sometimes call it "railroading."

Step Bombing

Advanced exercisers sometimes combine the two foregoing systems by starting with a weight with which they can do perhaps ten repetitions. After each rest period, five pounds is added. When they can perform only a single repetition, five pounds is removed between sets until they are back to the starting weight. Increasing the weight and decreasing the repetitions with each set is sometimes known as the pyramid system.

Blitz Program

The exerciser trains six days a week, but works on only a single body area each day. For instance, Monday and Thursday might be devoted to exercises for the arms and shoulders; Tuesdays and Fridays to the chest, upper back, and neck; and Wednesdays and Saturdays to the torso, lower back, and legs. In one popular routine, each exercise is performed for five sets of six repetitions each every hour or so. The goal is to keep a limited muscle area flushed with blood for a prolonged period. This is a very vigorous program and is usually followed for a comparatively short time. In effect, it is a split routine carried to an extreme. Usually comparatively light weights are employed.

Cheating Exercises

These exercises were introduced to American weight trainers by the German Olympic Weight Lifting Team at Los Angeles in 1932. They consist of using more weight than can be handled in strict form and then employing movements of other parts of the body (what kinesiologists term **synergistic muscle action**) to get the weight past the sticking point. In the two-hands curl, for instance, the problem is usually to get the weight started. Performed as a cheating exercise, the lifter leans forward at the waist and starts the lift by swinging the upper body backward. In the press, first the hips are swung backward and then the weight is started upward by swinging them forward. The essential point is that the movement is performed in proper style once the sticking point is surmounted.

This form of exercise has much to recommend it as it enables the lifter to provide maximal resistance to the muscle through that portion of the range of motion in which it is strongest, whereas otherwise the resistance afforded is actually controlled by the amount it can handle through the range wherein it is weakest. Further, it simultaneously exercises other parts of the body which would be involved to only a relatively small degree if the strict style were followed. The value of the exercise is lost if the synergistic movements are performed in such a way as to merely throw the weight through the movement. Properly performed, this is an extremely effective system.

Circuit (Sequence) Training

Strength and endurance may be improved by a program which places the emphasis on a reduction of the time required to complete a given exercise program. A circuit consists of a number of stations, at each of which one exercise is performed. The loads should be about one-half of one's maximal effort. A trial is given to see how long it takes to complete this series of exercises and then a target time is assigned approximately one-third faster than the recorded time. As soon as the person can complete the circuit in this time, the loads are increased; the exercise is timed again, and a new target time is established. Variations are possible in the number of exercises and the number of times one goes around the circuit. The circuit may be biased to give specialized or increased amounts of work to certain muscles or areas of the body.

This form of training is popular with athletes and the armed forces of the world (fig. 6.1) as it provides the cardiorespiratory stress which is lacking in most systems designed to develop strength. Its value has been confirmed scientifically in studies by Wilmore et al.[1] and by Gettman et al. It may be used in place of running programs, which are often plagued by boredom and, consequently, a high dropout rate. Some coaches consider circuit training the most valuable type of conditioning for swimmers.

Compound Exercises

Exercisers pressed for time may combine two exercises into one. For instance, do a curl or a reverse curl and continue the movement on into a press, or a press while executing a squat, or a deep knee bend followed by a heel raise, or a bent-arm pull-over followed by a press. This may have been the ancestor of the superset system, but possesses the disadvantage that the weight used will be governed by the amount which can be handled in the movement in which the person is weaker.

One system of weight training is referred to as cheating exercises. Why is this name appropriate, and what advantages are gained by these exercises?

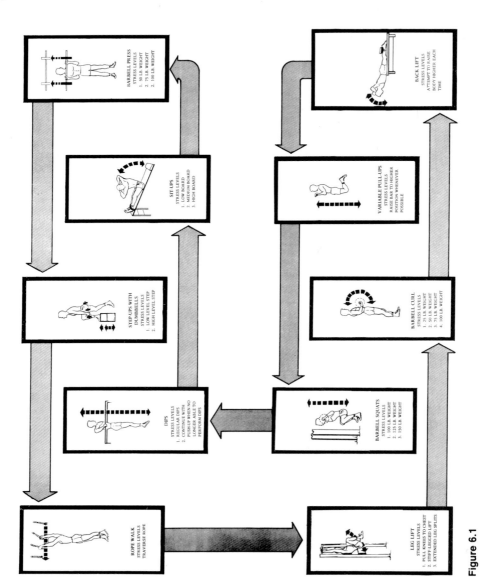

Figure 6.1

Standardized circuit used by the U.S. Marine Corps. The energy cost of circuit weight training is equivalent to that required for jogging at 5 mph.[1,2]

Peripheral Heart Action (PHA or Sequence) System

This is similar to some circuit training systems and is the opposite of the blitz program. The emphasis here is on keeping the blood in constant circulation through the muscular system so that it will bring a steady supply of oxygen, nourishment, and buffers to a given area, remove metabolic wastes, and prevent congestion. This is done by arranging groups of five or six exercises, called a **sequence,** in such a way that each exercise affects a different part of the body. For example, a sequence might consist of the press, rowing motion, sit-up, heel raise, and dead lift. Each exercise is performed for eight to ten repetitions, and each sequence is repeated two to five times. The exerciser then goes on to another sequence, performing in all a total of four to six sequences. No rest is taken between exercises or sequences; the exerciser goes right through one and into the next. Proponents of this system claim that they can take a heavier workout with less fatigue and quicker recovery, but generally concede that it is better adapted for producing strength and definition than muscular size.

Rest-Pause System

The weight trainer does a single movement or number of repetitions using close to his maximal weight, puts the weight down for a predetermined amount of time, does a second movement, rests, and repeats this process until the muscle is fatigued. This seems better fitted for the production of strength than hypertrophy.

Set System

The use of sets was introduced in the 1940s and is now by far the most popular advanced training method. Originally it was a variation of the heavy and light system—that is, in each set lighter weights than in the previous one were used. Now the trend is to keep the weight the same and to use fewer repetitions. The trainer does several repetitions of an exercise, rests, repeats the exercise, rests, and repeats it again. While the number of repetitions in a set and the number of sets may vary, there is some good evidence that three to four sets of approximately five to six repetitions each comprise the optimal combination for increasing strength. However, advanced exercisers often use two or three times as many sets. In order to conserve space, this would be indicated in a training schedule as 3 x 6, that is, three sets of six repetitions each. It seems doubtful that heavy loads with a few repetitions per set and a large number of sets are any more effective for improving strength than are lighter loads with more repetitions and fewer sets. MacQueen[3] recommends four or five sets of ten repetitions each for the development of hypertrophy. This is consistent with the findings of scientific studies to the effect that exercises of longer duration are followed by a greater increase in the volume of the muscle. Some experienced exercisers advocate doing each set at a different speed.

Supersets

A set of exercises for one group of muscles is followed immediately by a set for their antagonist. This alteration of contraction and extension movements is sometimes called the push-pull system. A variation of this is known as **super multiple sets** and consists of performing three sets of an exercise for one group of muscles, followed by the same number of sets for their antagonists. A short rest is taken between sets. Some experts consider this the most effective system for building the arms. These are extremely fatiguing methods and are recommended only for experienced individuals.

Split Routines

Individuals pressed for time or on a very heavy training program may pursue a split routine. This means that on one day they exercise only the upper body and the next day only the lower body. It is, of course, necessary to work out six days a week. Opinion is divided as to the desirability of this method. Some feel that it has no advantages over a normal program; others contend that a split program enables them to accomplish more exercise than they would otherwise without inducing overfatigue.

Burns

Some weight trainers follow their initial repetitions with a series of rapid half-contractions. This produces a burning sensation in the muscle—hence the name. They believe that this forces an additional amount of blood into the muscle and causes a greater increase in size. I know of no research study in which this theory has been evaluated.

Summary

There is little in the way of research material to indicate the comparative values of these programs and their numerous variations. Men like John Grimek (fig. 8.1) developed some of the great physiques of our time before blitz programs and other such methods were introduced. If the contemporary programs do nothing else, however, they introduce some welcome variety into training schedules which might otherwise become boring. Perhaps they serve to retain the interest of weight trainers who would otherwise fall by the wayside. Certainly they provide a fertile field of study for those interested in the scientific side of exercise.

Even with the best of systems, the average person may anticipate that the forearms and calves will prove difficult to develop, so do not become discouraged if they fail to respond as promptly as you would like. What has worked for someone else may or may not work for you. If you are not getting the results you think you should be, do not hesitate to experiment with other exercises, but give your new program sufficient time—say three months—to show its merits before abandoning it.

Which parts of the body are particularly difficult to develop for the average person?

Use of Apparatus

Barbells and dumbbells are often called "free weights" to distinguish them from weights used in conjunction with a piece of apparatus designed to control the course of their movement. During the last several years the weight trainers have developed a great deal of apparatus to help them attain maximal strength and hypertrophy. Some of it is ingenious but complicated and expensive; other pieces are simple and can be built by almost anyone.

Incline Bench (Slant Board)

One of the simplest and most common pieces of apparatus seen in weight-training gymnasia is the incline bench (fig. 6.2). This was originally designed so that the angle of the incline could be changed. The idea was that if it were slowly increased, the trainer would eventually be able to press in the standing position the same amount which was originally used in the bench press. This method of training seems to be largely forgotten. Most boards are now either built on a 45-degree slant or put in that position and left there so that the exerciser is in effect working in a position midway between supine and standing. It is especially valuable for pressing and flying motions, although curls and numerous other exercises can be performed on it with profit.

When a strap is fixed across the top so that the exerciser can insert the feet under it and place the head at the bottom, it is referred to as a decline board. Many individuals find a 45-degree incline too extreme and prefer to use one with a lesser gradient. Pressing done in this position is especially popular as it imparts a different stress to the pectorals and contributes to their full development.

Figure 6.2
Adjustable Incline Bench.

Figure 6.3
Athlete practicing seated preacher curls. Note that the subject is using a bar which has been bent much as described on page 26 so that the hands may be placed in an intermediate position. (Courtesy AMF American Athletic Equipment Division.)

Preacher Curl

This same type of apparatus is used for the preacher curl. The exerciser stands or sits behind an inclined board or pedestal, with the upper arms and elbows resting on a padded support (fig. 6.3). The forearms are extended until the arms are straight. The elbows are then flexed without permitting the upper arms and elbows to lose contact with the support. One respected gymnasium owner believes that these supports are usually too high. He recommends that their tops should be three inches lower than the bottom of the pectorals. The exercise is usually practiced with both the hands and the elbows about eleven inches apart or with the hands about three inches apart and the elbows about twenty.

Judging by the currently available evidence, how do the varieties of contemporary advanced exercise programs compare with one another in value? What advantage is there in becoming familiar with more than one program?

Hopper

The hopper is seldom seen in the gymnasium today, but in the writer's opinion it is an extremely valuable aid. The construction is diagrammed in figure 6.4 and can be built quite easily. In use, the exerciser stands in the center, lifts the barbell, and lets it come down hard so that the weight rebounds slightly. The hopper raises the bar high enough so that the period during which the upper body "hangs from its ligaments" during dead lifting is eliminated. This protects the lifter from back injuries. At the same time, the amount of weight which can be handled is considerably increased. It will be noted that use of this apparatus introduces the principle of "elastic rebound" into dead lifting.

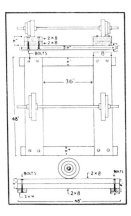

Figure 6.4
Diagram for construction of a hopper.

The disadvantages of this piece of apparatus are the thunderous noise and the shock which result when a heavy weight is banged down on it. It certainly has no place in an upstairs room if one has any regard for the plaster on the ceiling below. A rather ingenious solution to this problem was used by some of the earlier competitive dead lifters. These men dug a hole in the ground and stood in it while lifting the barbell. This enabled them to use a weight too heavy to be handled in the normal manner. As their strength increased, they began to fill in the hole, eventually arriving back at floor level. The basic idea, of course, is similar to the use of the adjustable incline board as a connecting link between the flat bench and the standing press. It would seem that the same thing could be more easily accomplished by lifting the weight from blocks and gradually decreasing their height.

Lat Machine

Probably the most popular piece of apparatus in the average gymnasium is the latissimus dorsi machine because of its demonstrated value in developing those muscles and thus producing the V-shape so admired by body builders (fig. 8.2). Normally, the person kneels or sits in front of it and pulls the bar down to his shoulders behind his head, although it is sometimes pulled down in front of the head as shown in figure 6.5. There are differently shaped bars, and they are said to have different effects on the muscles. Another popular exercise is to keep the elbows extended and swing the bar down in front of the body as though the arms were pivoted at the shoulders. A triceps extension movement is also popular. The bar is grasped with the forearms parallel to the floor. The elbows are then fully extended, with every effort being made to prevent any movement of the upper arms or body. This is usually called the triceps pull-down.

As his strength increases, a light man may find the weight tends to lift him up, and he may require a fixed seat with a belt attached to hold him in place.

A rather unusual exercise employing this piece of apparatus is curls performed while lying supine on the floor.

Figure 6.5
Lat Machine. (Photograph courtesy of Jubinville Health Equipment Company.)

Figure 6.6
Leg Press Machine. (Photograph courtesy of *Iron Man Magazine.*)

Leg Press Machine

Another popular piece of gymnasium equipment is the leg press machine (fig. 6.6). While it cannot be seen in figure 6.6, there is a small triangular platform which fits under and raises the hips, thereby flattening the lower back and reducing the chance of injury. It develops much the same muscles as does the squat, but a great deal more weight can be handled with this apparatus than in the squat, as it is not necessary to lift the body in addition to the weight. Research indicates that there is no significant difference between the strength gains resulting from the use of this apparatus and those resulting from the practice of squats.[4] From the biomechanical aspect, however, leg presses may be less specific to jumping than are squats and thus, not the exercise of choice for jumpers.

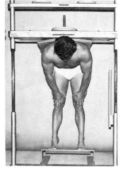

Figure 6.7
Donkey Raises. (Photographs courtesy of *Iron Man Magazine*.)

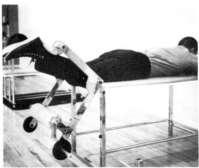

Figure 6.8
Knee Flexion and Extension Machine. (Photographs courtesy of Paramount Gymnasium Equipment Corp.)

A popular exercise for the calves performed with this machine is shown in figure 6.7. The exercise is known as the donkey raise and is illustrated so clearly that no explanation is required. The exercise can also be performed in the inverted position.

There are other machines designed to enable the exerciser to perform the same movements while seated. In these the bar rests on the tops of the thighs rather than on the shoulders.

Knee Flexion and Extension Machine

The uses of this machine are so well shown in figure 6.8 that there is no necessity for a description. Its great virtue is that it furnishes resistance throughout the range of movement. If prone knee flexion is performed with an iron boot, gravity takes over once the weight passes the perpendicular, and it then becomes a matter of contracting the extensors to keep it from falling on the exerciser. There is no other piece of apparatus known to me which quite replaces this item.

Figure 6.9
Jack Delinger, Mr. America 1949 and Mr. Universe 1956, exercising on a calf machine.
(Photograph courtesy of *Strength & Health.*)

Calf Machine

The calf machine comes in a large range of designs, but all are essentially ways of conveniently resting the resistance on the shoulders while doing heel raises. The example shown in figure 6.9 is one of the simpler models; some are engineered to work through a lever system. In any case, they are excellent devices for working these hard-to-develop muscles through their full range of movement.

Variable Resistance Machines

An example of a popular variable resistance machine is seen in figure 6.10. As has been explained earlier (see p. 2), this apparatus is designed to afford a relatively constant degree of resistance throughout the entire range of motion of a joint. When using a barbell, the exerciser is limited to the amount of weight that can be moved through the point of the poorest mechanical advantage. At all other points, the muscles are exercised at suboptimal levels. The variable resistance feature automatically compensates for changes in mechanical advantage and maintains a relatively stable load-to-strength ratio.

Almost any standard weight-training exercise can be practiced on these machines, and on some of them a number of individuals can work out at one time. The fact that the weights are under constant control is an important safety factor.

The research evidence generally indicates there is no significant difference in the results produced by variable resistance machines, constant resistance machines, and free weights.[4-12] One factor in favor of the use of free weights may be that they require the use of synergistic contractions to keep them from moving in undesired directions. Other possible explanations have been discussed by Stone, *et al.*[9] In general, machines impose movements less specific to those of sports than do free weights.

Can you recognize the following pieces of apparatus and describe their particular uses or values: leg press machine, variable resistance machine, incline bench, and lat machine?

Figure 6.10
A popular type of variable resistance apparatus. The cantilevers to which the weights are attached are designed to afford optimal resistance at point in the range of motion of a joint as alterations occur in the mechanical efficiency of the levers and the muscles which operate them. (Photograph courtesy of Universal Athletic Sales.)

Looking Ahead

In the future we may expect to see ever more complicated apparatus, the outcome of the application of the high-tech research to the development of musculature. The Triton Compensating Resistance Machine shown in figure 6.11 illustrates an application of advanced technology to the problem of changing the resistance while exercising. These machines utilize water as the resistance. A switch fitted to the index finger of the exerciser activates a pump which increases the quantity of water. When the switch is released, the water flows out at a rate claimed to be approximately equal to the decline in strength of the person exercising. In theory, at least, the muscle is being worked at its maximal strength capacity at each repetition. So far there seems to be no research reports on the effectiveness of this apparatus as compared with that of other equipment. It may be expected that more of this sort of apparatus will be developed as computers and other high-technology manufacturers seek new markets in the gymnasia. The prospective user should demand that the salesmen furnish copies of published research studies conducted by independent investigators before parting with money.

For an individual training in a sport, what is the advantage of free weights over machines?

Isometric Rack

The isometric rack is sometimes called the power rack. This name is inappropriate. As explained on page 6, power is equal to the work accomplished divided by the time required to do it. In isometric exercise, the bar is not moved, no work is accomplished, and the time is only rarely measured. While some use is made of isometric exercise as an adjunct to weight training, it is difficult to determine the extent to which it is actually employed. When it is utilized, the most common

Figure 6.11
Triton Compensating Resistance Machine. Currently, this is probably the outstanding example of high technology applied to progressive resistance exercise. (Photo courtesy of Ultra Performance Systems, Inc.)

Figure 6.12
Tommy Kono, who has held world weight lifting championships at two different weights, practicing isometric exercise at the sticking point in the two-hands press. (Photo courtesy of John Grimek.)

procedure seems to be to determine the sticking point in a given exercise. A bar is then fixed at this level, and the person exercises against it isometrically in hope of developing strength to the extent that an actual weight can be moved through this point (fig. 6.12). The writer knows of no research in which this method of training has been evaluated, and claims for its benefits must be treated with caution. This piece of apparatus may also be used to confine a barbell to a given range of movement, thus reducing the possibility of injury, but sacrificing the benefits of synergistic action.

Those who desire to experiment with the isometric rack as an aid in sports training might be interested in using a system such as the one devised by Bruno[13] for football players. The exercises consist of the squat, dead lift, bench press, and upright rowing motion. On Monday they are performed with the bar at a low level, on Wednesday with the bar at an intermediate level, and on Friday with the bar at a high level. Two sets of three to five repetitions are performed. The great drawbacks to this form of training are that it does nothing to improve cardiorespiratory condition, and there are very few sports which are specifically related to isometric exercise.

Negative (Eccentric) Exercise

In the last few years, negative (eccentric) exercise has received a good deal of attention as an advanced training technique. Much greater weights can be handled eccentrically than can be managed concentrically. While it is possible this form of exercise offers certain benefits, it also has certain drawbacks. The amount of weight which can be employed requires the assistance of training partners or the use of equipment which is heavy, expensive, and requires a good deal of space. There have been numerous reports of injuries and muscle soreness resulting from its practice. The explanation of this is controversial, but it probably results from either mechanical or ischemic damage to the muscle fibers. There is a serious question as to the extent to which negative exercise can reproduce the movements of work or sport.

Studies of the relative merits of concentric and eccentric exercise have been reviewed by Rasch[14] and by Nelson.[15] A number of different programs and types of equipment have been employed, but differences have seldom been observed in the effects of the two techniques on muscular strength and hypertrophy. There is some evidence that it is less effective than concentric exercise in the development of strength.

References

1. Wilmore, Jack, *et al.* 1978. Physiological alterations consequent to circuit weight training. *Medicine and Science in Sports* 10:79–84.
2. Gettman, Larry R., *et al.* 1982. A comparison of combined running and weight training with circuit weight training. *Medicine and Science in Sports and Exercise* 14:229–34.
3. MacQueen, I. J. 1954. Recent Advances in the Technique of Progressive Resistance Exercise. *British Medical Journal* 2:1193–98.
4. Burleson, Larry A. 1969. Two Types of Weight Training Exercise and Their Relationship of Leg Strength Development Among Selected Male Students at Chico State College, 1968. Unpublished Graduate Study. Chico State College.
5. Pipes, Thomas V. 1978. Variable Resistance Versus Constant Resistance Strength Training in Adult Males. *European Journal of Applied Physiology* 39:27–35.
6. Stiggins, Charles F. 1978. Nautilus and Free Weight Training Program: A Comparison of Strength Development at Four Angles in the Range of Motion. Unpublished Master's Thesis. Brigham Young University.
7. Sanders, Michael T. 1980. A Comparison of Two Methods of Training on the Development of Muscular Strength and Endurance. *Journal of Orthopaedic and Sports Physical Therapy* 1:210–13.
8. Coleman, A. Eugene. 1977. Nautilus vs. Universal Gym Strength Training in Adult Males. *American Corrective Therapy Journal* 31:103–07.
9. Stone, Michael H., *et al.* 1979. A Short-Term Comparison of Two Different Methods of Resistance Training on Leg Strength and Power. *Athletic Training* 14:158–60.
10. Buckbee, Bruce E. 1981. The Effects of Selected Resistance Training Equipment and Regimens on Strength in College Age Women. Unpublished Doctoral Dissertation. Springfield College.

11. Rankin, Susan Ruth. 1981. A Comparison of the Use of Nautilus Apparatus and Universal Gym Equipment for the Development of Strength and Flexibility. Unpublished Master's Thesis. Pennsylvania State University.

12. Shields, Clarence L., Jr., *et al.* 1985. Comparison of Leg Strength Training Equipment. *Physician and Sportsmedicine* 13:49–56.

13. Bruno, Frederick W. 1972. Power Rack Training for Football. *Athletic Journal* 53 *et seq.*

14. Rasch, Philip J. 1974. The Present Status of Negative (Eccentric) Exercise: A Review. *American Corrective Therapy Journal* 28:77 *et seq.*

15. Nelson, Arnold C. 1977. A Comparison of the Effects of Maximal Eccentric and Orthodox Weight Training on Muscular Hypertrophy, Muscular Strength, and Muscular Power. Unpublished Master's Thesis. Brigham Young University.

The Use of Dumbbells

7

In the present day gymnasia the use of dumbbells is all but ignored. This is unfortunate, as most "old timers" believe they have special merits of their own. Nearly any exercise that can be done with a barbell can be duplicated with dumbbells. The latter frequently also have special advantages. Often they create more stress on the muscles than do the barbells. In the press, for instance, the even distribution of the weight on a barbell tends to inhibit any tendency for the bar to move sideways, whereas dumbbells require a powerful contraction of the shoulder muscles to keep them from dropping to the sides. Few individuals can press as much with two dumbbells as they can with one barbell. In the curl, the bar inhibits the tendency of the biceps to turn the forearms into a supine position. Most men, nevertheless, prefer barbells to dumbbells. Among the older weight trainers, the latter have a reputation for making a person stiff. The reason for this was never clear to me, and I have not personally experienced this effect. Unfortunately, researchers have ignored the study of dumbbell training, and we have no real information on its value as compared with barbell exercises. Training with dumbbells, however, has been found to be as effective in developing elbow flexor strength as is training on the Nautilus Omni Biceps Machine.[1]

In routine exercises such as the press and the curl most trainers seem to prefer "alternate" exercises—that is, one arm goes up as the other is coming down. Usually more weight can be handled in this way than when both are pressed or curled together, and it is easier to concentrate on the movement being made. There is, however, a decided tendency to use body movements to aid the arms. To avoid this, many prefer to do such exercises either sitting or on the incline bench. While I have no scientific evidence to back up my opinion, I have a strong impression that a number of bodybuilders famed for the girth of their arms spend an inordinate amount of time working with duimbbells either seated or on the incline bench.

While barbell exercises can be done with dumbbells, it does not follow that the reverse is true. There are a number of dumbbell exercises which cannot be performed with a barbell. Some of the more popular are described here.

Front Raise

Stand erect, with the dumbbells resting against the front of the thighs, elbows extended, palms in; raise them to shoulder height directly in front, swing the arms back until they are parallel to the shoulders, and then lower them to the

Figure 7.1
Front Raise. (Photographs by Gene Mozee.)

Figure 7.2
Bent Over Lateral Raise.

sides. Next lift them back to shoulder height, swing them to the forward position, and lower them to the original starting position (fig. 7.1). The elbows must be kept extended throughout the exercise.

A variation is to start the movements by raising the arms until the dumbbells are overhead and then lowering them to shoulder height. Another variation is to lean forward at the waist, the arms hanging down, and then raise the dumbbells as high as possible while keeping them in line with the shoulders (fig. 7.2). This is known as the **bent over lateral raise.** These exercises develop the shoulders and upper back: deltoids, supraspinatus, upper trapezius, and associated muscle groups.

A **side raise,** done while lying on one side on a bench, is also popular.

Why do "alternate" exercises seem to be preferred when doing the press and curl or other routine dumbbell exercises? What should you be careful to avoid as the up and down actions of the arms are alternated?

Figure 7.3
Dumbbell Swing. (Photographs by Gene Mozee.)

Dumbbell Swing

The exerciser bends over with the elbows extended and the dumbbell held between the legs with both hands, knees semiflexed. The dumbbell is swung upward, keeping the elbows extended. The feet do not move, but the exerciser comes to a semierect position (fig. 7.3). One variation is to swing the dumbbell in one hand, with the free hand placed on the knee. The hands may be changed at the top of the swing so that the swing is made with each hand alternately. Another is to swing the dumbbell up and to squat or to take a lunging step forward at the same time. A dumbbell may be used in each hand, starting them outside the legs and swinging them both at once.

While these variations affect the body in somewhat different ways, the general purpose is to develop the muscles of the lower back: the spinae erectors and associated muscle groups. The shoulders, especially the deltoids, also benefit. Dumbbell swings must not be done until the exerciser is well warmed up, or back strain may be suffered.

Flying Motion

The exerciser is supine on a flat bench, arms extended in line with the shoulders but partially flexed at the elbows. The arms are crossed over the chest and then returned to the starting position. The arms are alternated each time they are crossed so that one is uppermost one time and the other the next (fig. 7.4).

A variation of this is to do the exercise with the elbows straight. This is known as the **supine** or **straight-arm lateral raise** and is open to the same objection as is the straight-arm pull-over. Either form, however, develops the shoulders and upper chest and back: deltoids, pectoralis major, middle trapezius, and associated muscle groups.

Figure 7.4
Flying Motion. (Photographs by Gene O'Connell.)

Hise Deltoid Exercise

The exerciser grasps a doorway or some other brace with one hand. The arm is extended, but with most individuals there is a slight bend in the elbow, and the torso is usually at a slight angle backward. The exercise starts with the weight overhead, elbow extended and upper arm close to the head, as though a press had just been completed. The dumbbell is lowered rapidly to the shoulder and at once rebounded to arm's length. The supporting arm prevents body movement which might aid in the exercise and relieves the exerciser from any worries about retaining balance. The collars must be set up tightly as the rapid rebounding will tend to loosen them. As the name indicates, this exercise is designed primarily to influence the deltoids, but the triceps and upper shoulder muscle groups in general benefit from it. It will be noted that this is another example of "elastic rebound" training.

Such rebound or counter-movements form the basis of **plyometric** training. A somewhat oversimplified explanation of the underlying theory of this system is as follows: All skeletal muscles contain organs called muscle spindles. These detect deviations from positions of balance and react to correct them by initiating a protective contraction of the antagonistic muscles. This is termed a *stretch reflex*. The spindles are affected by both the amount and the speed of the stretching. The faster a muscle is stretched and the greater the amount of the stretching, the more forceful the following contraction of the antagonists, and consequently, the greater the resistance that can be overcome. Whether this deliberate invocation of the stretch reflex has a useful role in strength training remains to be demonstrated.

One-Arm Push

The exerciser stands erect with the dumbbell at the shoulder and the opposite foot a little advanced. As the weight is pushed up, the hand turns so that the palm is rotated forward, almost on a line with the shoulders, the knees are flexed a little, the torso bends forward and is supported by the free forearm coming to rest on the knee of the advanced leg. The hip on the lifting side must be thrust backward as a counterbalance. Most lifters find it easier to control the weight if

Figure 7.5
Side Bend. (Photographs by Tony Takash.)

they look upward at it. Many prefer to put their free hand on the advanced knee as they begin to lean forward and then slide the forearm across it. In this way they are never left unsupported. The weight is kept a little back of the center line of the body.

This exercise is excellent for practically all of the muscles of the shoulder and back as well as for the arm extensors. In an advanced form, this movement develops into the **bent press.** This is now an almost forgotten lift, but when it was in its heyday, a good bent presser could put up as much weight with one arm in this style as he could press with both arms in the usual manner.

Side Bend

The exerciser stands erect, the dumbbell at the side, bends as far to that side as possible, and then returns to the erect position (fig. 7.5). This movement exercises the lateral flexors: abdominis oblique, erector spinae, and associated muscle groups.

Wrist Abduction

The dumbbell is loaded at one end. The exerciser stands erect, arms at the sides or with the free arm on the hip, and grasps the weight by the free end. Drop the wrist as far as possible and then cock it up as high as possible (fig. 7.6). This exercises the forearm abductors: flexor carpi radialis, extensor carpi radialis, and associated muscle groups.

Wrist Adduction

The dumbbell is loaded as before, but grasped so that the weight is to the back instead of forward. The movement is made through the full range of movement.

Figure 7.6
Wrist Abduction. (Photographs by Tony Takash.)

This exercises the forearm adductors: flexor carpi ulnaris, extensor carpi ulnaris, and associated muscle groups. This exercise and the preceding one are said to be beneficial in the prevention of tennis elbow.

Can you describe the theory underlying plyometric exercise? What is currently known about the value of rebound exercise in weight training?

Forearm Supination-Pronation

The exerciser sits with one forearm on his or her knee as for wrist curls, the hand holding a dumbbell. The forearm is rotated from full supination to full pronation. This works the forearm supinators and pronators: biceps, supinator, pronator quadratus, and associated muscle groups. A variation is to grip the free end of a dumbbell loaded at the other and to supinate and pronate the forearm.

Zottman Curl

The exerciser either stands erect or bends over at the waist, with a dumbbell held between the legs and the free hand on the knee. Curl the weight, pronate the forearm, and lower the weight to the starting point. It is then reverse curled to the chest, the forearm is supinated, and the weight is lowered again (fig. 7.7). The amount of weight that can be handled in this exercise will, of course, be controlled by the degree of strength which can be exerted in the reverse curl. This is an excellent exercise for the elbow flexors and the forearm supinators and pronators: biceps, brachialis, brachioradialis, supinator, pronator quadratus, and associated muscle groups.

Figure 7.7
Steps in the Zottman Curl. (Photographs by Gene O'Connell.)

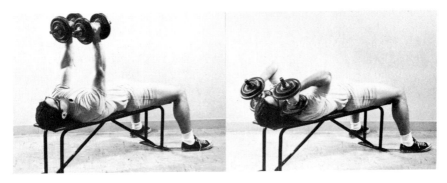

Figure 7.8
Triceps Extension on Bench with Dumbbells. (Photographs by Gene O'Connell.)

Triceps Extension on Bench with Dumbbells

This exercise will be recognized as a variation on the standard method of using a barbell in the standing position as described in chapter 4. The exerciser lies on the back on a bench, both arms fully extended upward, as though completing a supine press with dumbbells. While the upper arms are kept elevated, the elbows are flexed and then extended (fig. 7.8). Like the barbell exercise, the effect is largely on the elbow extensors: the triceps.

Dumbbell High Pull-Up

The exerciser assumes a lunge position, with the dumbbell close to the forward foot. Pull it as nearly as possible straight up, ending in a position somewhat similar to that of a high pull-up (fig. 7.9). Care must be taken that the hand is not turned over and the weight pressed into the final position. This is an excellent exercise for the arm flexors and upper shoulder muscles: biceps, brachialis, brachioradialis, deltoids, supraspinatus, trapezius, and associated muscle groups.

Figure 7.9
Steps in Dumbbell High Pull-Up. (Photographs by Gene Mozee.)

Figure 7.10
Concentration Triceps Extension Exercise. (Photographs by Gene Mozee.)

Concentration Exercises

The basic idea underlying concentration exercises is to employ a movement which insofar as possible is restricted to the use of a given muscle group, to stabilize the joint so that accessory muscle movement is eliminated, and then to focus one's full concentration on the muscle group being exercised. How important the concentration factor is we do not know. Generally such exercises are done with a dumbbell as it is difficult to secure the required stabilization when using a barbell. Figure 7.10 shows the triceps extension exercise done as a concentration exercise. You will observe that the free hand is used to firmly anchor the weight-bearing arm alongside the ear, thus ensuring that the exercise is done without aid from accessory muscles or body movement. Having only to think of relaxing and contracting the triceps, the exerciser is free to concentrate on this one muscle. Alternatively, this exercise may be done using both hands to hold the dumbbell, with the little fingers against one end of the grip.

Figure 7.11
Concentration Curl. (Photograph by Gene Mozee.)

Concentration Curl

Perhaps the most common exercise of this type is the concentration curl. Sit with the elbow firmly braced against the leg, as shown in figure 7.11. It is kept in this position during the entire movement. A variation is to sit in a chair, keeping one's back in contact with the back of the chair throughout the entire movement.

Another technique is to lie prone on a bench with the arms hanging down over the edge of the bench and to do curls while the edge of the bench prevents any backward movement of the arms. This is frequently shown in magazine articles, but is attended by difficulties in performance. Unless the bench is comparatively high off the floor, it will not be possible to extend the elbows fully. The average bench is designed primarily for bench presses and is too narrow for this sort of curling. Finally, the edge of the bench cuts into the triceps and is extremely uncomfortable.

The Concentration Dumbbell Rowing Motion

This exercise is shown in figure 7.12. Actually, the body is not too well braced in this position, and some care is required to make sure that the movement is not assisted by rotation of the torso.

There are, of course, other concentration exercises, but all work on the same principle—that is, of isolating the action of a muscle or a muscle group to as complete an extent as is possible.

Is there a limit to the possible development of strength in a given individual? If so, what determines the potential level?

Figure 7.12
Concentration Dumbbell Rowing Motion. (Photographs by Gene Mozee.)

Iron Boot

The iron boot is simply a device for attaching a dumbbell to the feet. The most common exercises performed with it are the following.

1. Standing—knee flexion, straight-leg raise in front, in back, and to the side.
2. Sitting—knee extension. It should be mentioned that many therapists discourage use of this exercise as a means of restoring strength to an injured knee, as they believe the weight tends to pull the joint apart when the knee is at the 90° angle. They prefer to use a machine such as is shown in figure 6.8 or one in which a cable is attached to the shoe and runs under the seat to the weight holder, thus relieving the knee of the need for supporting the resistance.
3. Supine lying—leg raise with knee straight, leg spread, inverted bicycle ride.
4. Prone lying—knee flexion. It should be noted that such leg curls have been suspected of damaging the knee when a position of deep flexion is assumed. Consequently, many strength coaches keep the resistance at a low level in this exercise.
5. Side lying—leg raising.

References

1. Stiggins, Charles F. 1978. Nautilus and free weight training program: A comparison of strength development at four angles in the range of motion. Unpublished Master's Thesis. Brigham Young University.

On Taking
Measurements

8

Weight trainers are quite likely to talk of the value of exercise for health and physical fitness, but to be interested primarily in the girth of their muscles. There is probably no type of recording in the entire field of physical activity so subject to exaggeration, not to say downright mendacity, as the reported physical measurements of bodybuilders. Peary Rader, former editor of *Iron Man,* has observed that it is next to impossible to obtain valid measurements from most of the top body-builders. "If you were to ask them their measurements," he commented, "they may tell you something, but it will not be a very factual measurement. The only recent factual measurements of bodybuilders or weight lifters were the ones taken by Willoughby at the recent Stong Men Contest in California."[1] Why these men deliberately choose to reflect discredit on their sport and themselves is difficult to explain, but one should look with great suspicion upon the alleged measurements of any contestant who is not willing to have them taken by competent anthropometrists. It is strange indeed that the Mr. America anthropometric data have been permitted to rest upon nothing better than the word of the men concerned—some of whom have proved uncooperative—whereas a lifter is required to use weights checked and certified by competent weighers using tested scales.

There are standard techniques for taking anthropometric measurements, and they must be followed exactly by anyone not deliberately desiring to deceive. It is necessary that all measuring be done by a second person as it is almost impossible for a man to measure himself and be sure that the tape does not slant up, down, or sideways. Measurements must be taken BEFORE, not AFTER, exercise. The data desired are the normal sizes, not the temporary girths of muscles swollen by vigorous activity. A flexible steel tape should be used, preferably one marked off in tenths of an inch rather than in the usual sixteenths. The tape is laid on the skin and pulled snug but not tight. If too loose, it will give figures which are too large; if pulled so tightly as to cut into the flesh, it will give readings which are too small. Be certain that no fingers are under the tape. This warning may seem ludicrous, but it is not an unusual situation when the circumference of the chest is being determined. Actually both sides of the body should be measured and reported, but it is the general custom to give only one figure—which, of course, may be assumed to be the one more favorable to the individual in question. Height must be taken barefoot and weight in the nude.

The regulations governing the AAU Mr. America competition as set forth in the 1983 *Official Physique Manual* are vague and incomplete. There is no information on the goals of the contest and no requirement that contestants demonstrate their ability to do anything with their muscles. The observer is left to wonder why so much effort has been spent on developing them if they are not used. No provision is made for obtaining and recording anthropometric data. A subcommittee is charged with developing and administering a program of drug testing, but there is no provision for required reports and their publication.

There is no "official" set of prescribed measurements, but most of the recommendations made by Willoughby[2] more than forty years ago have been generally accepted and comprise the present practice. Instructions for the measurements ordinarily reported in male physique contests are as follows:

Neck—The head is erect, eyes looking forward, neck muscles relaxed. The measurement is made at the smallest girth, just above the Adams's apple.

Upper arm—The arm is raised to shoulder height and the elbow flexors are fully contracted, palm down, fist clenched and turned down. The girth is taken at the point of greatest size of the biceps. The tape must be at right angles to the upper arm bone (humerus).

Forearm—The arm is straight, with no bend at the wrist, and held at an angle away from the body. The fist is clenched so that the forearm muscles are fully contracted. The taping is made below the elbow at the point of greatest girth.

Wrist—The palm is held up, fingers extended in line with the forearm. The measurement is made at the point between the base of the hand and the bony protuberance on the little finger side of the hand (styloid process of the ulna).

Chest normal—The body is erect, the head up, breathing normal. The circumference is taken at the largest part. The tape is placed just above the nipples in front and must be straight across the back. The measurer must check carefully to make sure that the subject is not contracting the latissimus dorsi.

Chest expanded—The tape is kept in the same position as for Chest normal while the subject inhales deeply and expands his chest to its greatest size. Again, care must be taken to see that he does not flex the latissimus dorsi in the process. One occasionally sees advertisements claiming that someone has a chest expansion of ten inches or so and can develop the same amount in those who take his course. Expansions of this kind are not typical of the experienced weight trainer. If the expanded chest measurement of such an individual exceeds the normal chest measurement by more than two or three inches, it must be carefully rechecked as the tape has probably slipped or muscle contraction has been included. Neither is there the slightest evidence that increasing the chest expansion in this manner will double one's life expectancy, as is often claimed.

Waist—The body is erect, the abdominal muscles in a normal state of tonus. The waist is measured at the smallest part, usually a little above the navel. The abdomen must not be sucked in, although figures are often cited which suggest very strongly that this is exactly what has occurred.

Thigh—The body is erect, feet about six inches apart, weight equally distributed on each foot, and thigh muscles relaxed. Measurement is made at the largest part, usually just below the buttocks.

Calf—The body is erect, with heels on the floor, the weight equally distributed on each foot. The measurement is taken at the largest girth.

Ankle—The body is erect, with the heels on the floor and the weight equally distributed on each foot. Measurement is made at the smallest part, usually about two inches above the ankle bones (lateral and medial malleolus).

In the present craze for sheer bulk, bodybuilders frequently lose sight of the fact that the individual measurements must be in proportion if the result is to be harmonious—that is, the potential physique contest winner must be not only well developed, but also symmetrical in appearance. For some reason bodybuilders have concentrated on the image of huge arms. The results have often resulted in a disproportionate body development. More losers in physique contests suffer from the fact that their legs seem underdeveloped in comparison with their arms and upper body than from the other way around.

What is the average American male physique and what sort of development must a man attain if he is to have a chance to win in topnotch competition? After careful study of the research materials Willoughby concluded that the typical male college freshman has the measurements shown in table 8.1. These data may be compared with those of the "ideal" as represented by the averages of the measurements claimed by the Mr. Americas from 1940 through 1980.

Can you recommend changes in the rules for the AAU Mr. America competition that would improve the status of this event?

In recent years the trend has been away from performance and toward display. In general physique, winners tend to have comparatively small bones, joints, waists, hips, and buttocks, combined with broad shoulders and a comparatively huge chest (figs. 8.2 and 8.3). The lifters are more likely to have comparatively big bones, a relatively long trunk, short arms and legs, a thick waist, and well-developed buttocks. At age 36, Merited Master of Sport, Vasily Alexeyev (fig. 8.4), Superheavyweight Weight Lifting Champion from 1970–1978, was 6′ 2″ tall and weighed 350 lbs. His neck measured 22″, chest normal 56″, chest expanded 59″, upper arms 20-¼″, waist 62″, thigh 34″, and calf 19″. While Alexeyev's waist measurement is exceptionally large, his other girths are typical of the modern giants of strength. For comparative purposes, measurements recorded by Willoughby[3] at the 1980 World's Strongest Man contest are shown in table 8.2. Mr. Americas may, of course, demonstrate impressive strength when the amounts of weight used in their training exercises are taken as the criteria (fig. 8.5), but they are seldom noted for brute strength and men who are do not usually win physique contests. Bodybuilders tend to be larger in the chest, arms, and forearms than do Olympic lifters, but physiologically, they fit into the average nonathletic population (fig. 8.1).

Table 8.1.   Anthropometry of American Men

Measurement	Average College Freshman	Average 1940–1980 Mr. America	Average World's Strongest
Height	69.00''	68.78''	74.75''
Neck	14.80''	17.50''	20.50''
Chest normal	37.80''	48.81''	56.95''
Chest expanded		50.78''	
Upper arm	12.95''	18.52''	20.32''
Forearm	11.20''	13.99''	16.25''
Wrist	7.04''	7.61''	8.82''
Waist	31.45''	31.08''	
Hips	37.20''		
Thigh	21.40''	26.10''	30.97''
Knee			14.90''
Calf	14.50''	17.19''	18.65''
Ankle	8.92''	9.65''	11.25''
Weight	155 lbs.	203 lbs.	324 lbs.

(David P. Willoughby)

Figure 8.1
John C. Grimek, Mr. America 1940–41, Mr. USA 1948, Mr. Universe 1948, and considered by many authorities to possess the most perfect male physique of all time, is a former National and North American Weight Lifting Champion. He was a member of the 1936 Olympic team and represented the United States in the World Weight Lifting Championships in 1938. This athlete competed in both the light heavyweight and the heavyweight divisions. He has held various national records. His left-hand clean and jerk as a heavyweight still stands. Grimek is the only Mr. Universe who was never beaten in physique competition.

Figure 8.2

Steve Reeves, Mr. America 1947. Many fans still consider Reeves to have been the greatest example of the V shape in the history of physique contests. (Courtesy *Iron Man Magazine*.)

Figure 8.3

Chris Dickerson, Mr. USA 1968, Amateur Mr. Universe 1973, Professional Mr. Universe 1974. In 1970, Dickerson made history by becoming the first black to achieve Mr. America honors. He is particularly noted for his calf development. Dickerson has won more titles than any other bodybuilder in history, including Amateur Mr. Universe 1972, Professional Mr. America and Professional Mr. Universe 1974, and Mr. Olympia 1982. He is the only Mr. America–Mr. Olympia winner in history.

Figure 8.4

Vasily Alexeyev exemplifies the barrel-like physique characteristic of the giants of strength. By the time of his retirement in 1980, he had set 82 world records, including a clean and jerk of 563.2 lbs. and a two lift total of 979 lbs.

Table 8.2 Anthropometric Measurements of Certain Competitors in the 1980 World's Strongest Man Contest

Name	Height (Inches)	Weight (Pounds)	Neck	Chest Normal (Inches)	Arm	Fore-arm	Wrist	Thigh	Calf	Ankle
Bill Kazmaier	6'2"	320	22.0	58.5	21.5	17.0	8.8	31.5	20.4	11.0
Don Reinhoudt	6'3"	345	20.0	59.5	20.0	17.2	9.4	31.5	19.0	11.5
Lars Hedlund	6'3"	315	18.7	56.0	18.7	15.1	8.0	29.2		
Jon Kolb	6'3"	254	18.1	49.7	18.0	14.5		27.5	18.1	
Doug Young	5'10.5"	265	21.2	56.0	20.5	15.7	7.7	29.1	17.1	
Cleve Dean	6'7"	450	23.0	62.0	23.2	18.0	10.2	37.0		

Figure 8.5
Val Vasilieff, Mr. America 1964, in a relaxed pose rather than in a tensed pose, as usually assumed by physique contestants. Willoughby (in the **Super Athletes,** p. 167) credits Vasilieff with a correct two-hands curl of 220 lbs., a press of 315 lbs., a snatch of 270 lbs., a clean and jerk of 360 lbs., a bench press of 450 lbs., and a two-hands dead lift of 600 lbs.—rather convincing evidence that shapeliness and strength can be combined.

As physique contests increased in popularity, other entrepreneurs organized rival exhibitions, awarded the same title to the winners, and began publicizing them accordingly. This has been the source of a great deal of confusion. Since 1977, however, amateurs from the International Federation of Body Builders have been permitted to participate in the AAU Mr. America competitions and vice versa. Possibly this will eventually result in a single Mr. America.

At the international level, the most prestige is attached to the Mr. Universe competition, held in London each year, and the Mr. Olympia contest. Unfortunately, contestants rarely participate in both events, so we lack the head-to-head comparisons necessary to determine a true international champion.

What probable differences in musculature distinguish successful physique competitors from the average man? Do these differences imply that it is or is not realistic for the average man to aspire to the measurements of a Mr. America?

Successful physique competitors probably possess muscles usually absent in the average individual and there is some evidence that they have a greater number of muscle fibers. It is, of course, totally unrealistic for the average man to hope to attain the measurements claimed by the Mr. Americas. A much more rational approach is for him to set as his goal attainment of a physique which is both well developed and well balanced, even if not as massive as that of physique contest winners. On the basis of over fifty years of observation and study of well-developed athletes and bodybuilders, Willoughby has devised a chart on which an individual can plot his measurements and determine the symmetry of his body. With this information available, he can determine at a glance which parts require specialized training and evaluate the results of such training over short or long periods of time. Table 8.3 is a considerably abridged version of the Willoughby chart.

Curiously enough, the Soviets strongly encourage weightlifting, but violently denounce bodybuilding as "alien to the Soviet notion of physical education." They portray it as a Western creation which originated in England and then spread to the United States. However, participation in this activity is rumored to be increasing in spite of official disapproval.

A further word of explanation about the Mr. America title might clarify the picture for the newcomer to the field of weight training. Apparently the title is not copyrighted, and the idea of using it occurred independently to two entrepreneurs in 1939. In connection with the AAU weightlifting championships in Chicago that year, a board of artists and other aesthetes selected the handsome but underdeveloped Roland Essmaker as Mr. America. That same year Bert Goodrich, a worthy choice, was awarded the same title in an Amsterdam, New York, contest. In 1940, competition was held on a truly national basis and was won by John C. Grimek. When he repeated his triumph the following year and appeared likely to continue to do so indefinitely, a rule was passed prohibiting a winner from competing in future contests.

Table 8.3. Willoughby Symmetrometer

Status of Ratio or Measurement	Minimum		Small					Medium				Large						Maximum		
Weight ÷ Height →	1.6	1.7	1.8	1.9	2.0	2.1	2.2	2.3	2.4	2.5	2.6	2.7	2.8	2.9	3.0	3.1	3.2	3.3	3.4	3.5	3.6
Neck		13.0		14.0			15.0		16.0			17.0			18.0			19.0			
Biceps, R.	12.1		13.0			14.0			15.0		16.0			17.0		18.0					
„ L.		12.0		13.0			14.0		15.0			16.0			17.0		18.0				
Forearm, R.	10.1		11.0			12.0			13.0			14.0			15.0						
„ L.		10.0		11.0			12.0		13.0			14.0			15.0						
Wrist, R.		6.0				6.5		7.0			7.5			8.0			8.5				
„ L.			6.0			6.5		7.0			7.5			8.0			8.5				
Chest (normal)		34.0	35.0	36.0	37.0	38.0	39.0	40.0	41.0	42.0	43.0	44.0	45.0	46.0	47.0	48.0	49.0	50.0	51.0		
Waist	25.0	26.0	27.0	28.0	29.0	30.0	31.0		32.0	33.0	34.0	35.0		36.0		37.0		38.0			
Hips	30.0	31.0	32.0	33.0	34.0	35.0	36.0	37.0	38.0	39.0	40.0	41.0	42.0	43.0	44.0	45.0	46.0				
Thigh, R.	18.0		19.0		20.0	21.0	22.0	23.0		24.0		25.0		26.0		27.0					
„ L.	18.0		19.0		20.0	21.0	22.0	23.0		24.0		25.0		26.0		27.0					
Knee, R.		12.0		13.0			14.0			15.0			16.0			17.0		18.0			
„ L.		12.0		13.0			14.0			15.0			16.0			17.0		18.0			
Calf, R.	12.0		13.0			14.0			15.0			16.0			17.0			18.0			
„ L.	12.0		13.0			14.0			15.0			16.0			17.0			18.0			
Ankle, R.	7.0		7.5			8.0		8.5		9.0			9.5			10.0			10.5		
„ L.	7.0		7.5			8.0		8.5		9.0			9.5			10.0			10.5		

(Girths)

Instructions: Make the required measurements according to the directions given earlier in chapter 8 and plot the data on the appropriate scales by making heavy dots at the proper points. Plot the larger of the two arms as the right arm, regardless of whether it is actually the right or the left, and vice versa. Connect the dots by means of a heavy line. The more nearly this coincides with a line drawn perpendicularly from the Weight/Height point to the bottom of the chart, the more symmetrical are the proportions of the body. A variation of ±2.5 percent is acceptable. To help in visualizing these limits, parallel lines may be drawn at 1.05 and 0.95 percent of the Weight/Height figure. In obese individuals, body weight will take care of itself if the oversized areas, particularly the waist, are brought into line with the other girth measurements, particularly the wrists and ankles. (Copyright by David P. Willoughby. Reproduced by special permission.)

References

1. *Iron Man* 39:38. 1980.
2. David P. Willoughby. 1944. *How to Take Your Measurements.* Montreal: Your Physique Publishing Co.
3. David P. Willoughby. October-November 1979. An Anthropometrist's Paradise. *Iron Man* 39:18 *et seq.*

Weight Training for Athletes

9

The value of strength and muscular development depends upon what you can do with it. Yet there are few questions in the field of physical training which are more controversial than the relationship between increases in strength and gains in performance. For every thesis or published study reporting that the practice of progressive resistance exercises improved performance in swimming, running, jumping, or some other activity there is another study stating that no such benefits could be observed. Over 25 years ago Pierson and Rasch concluded:

> The role of strength in motor performance is not clear, the effect of
> strength development in conditioning to the rigors of an activity is con-
> jectural, and the evidence concerning the relationships of strength, body
> size, and composition is contradictory.[1]

The picture is not much clearer today. Obviously a certain amount of strength is necessary for successful participation in any sport. Once this level is reached, further gains in strength do not appear to be accompanied by equivalent increases in performance. The optimal strength levels for various forms of activity are not known, however, and it is probably safe to assume that most athletes will profit by developing more than they have (fig. 9.1). The practice of a sport only improves strength up to the amount required to execute the basic movements of that activity. It is necessary for the athlete to pursue a program specifically designed to increase strength if he or she is to get stronger. Some strength coaches believe an athlete must train with loads greater than 80 percent of his maximum capacity if optimal increases are to be achieved.

The school or club athlete will, of course, train under the direction of a coach. This chapter is not designed to interfere with that relationship. In a booklet of this size the coverage of a given sport must necessarily be superficial and incomplete. However, it will serve to give readers an idea of the programs being utilized by those most closely connected with certain areas of athletics today. Those interested in a specific activity should have no problem in finding a specialty text which discusses training techniques in greater detail than is feasible here. It should be pointed out that there are a number of pitfalls in designing weight-training programs for athletes. Those charged with this responsibility should not fail to read Jesse's[2] discussion of these possible problems.

Figure 9.1
Ronald Lacy, Mr. America and Most Muscular 1957. Lacy attended college on a football scholarship and earned letters in three sports.

Football

Weight-training programs for professional and many college teams have become so incredibly complex that it is no longer possible to discuss them in a booklet of this length. They may be varied according to the time of the year, the day of the week, the position played, the player's physical status, the demands of the schedule, and other factors. They may involve both free weights (fig. 9.2) and several pieces of expensive equipment. In some cases each player is presented with individualized computer printouts which list the weights and repetitions to be employed in his exercise program during a given period. Training in one of the martial arts may be integrated with the use of weights. Those desiring to familiarize themselves with such schedules will find them described in articles in the *National Strength & Conditioning Journal.* Here we can do no more than present a few of the simpler programs which might be utilized in the weight rooms of the average high school, college, or university.

At the University of Alabama the basic off-season strength training program consists of:

	Sets	Reps.
Parallel Squats	4	8
Incline or Bench Press	4	8
Power Cleans	8	5
Neck Exercises	1	10

Figure 9.2
University of Texas football players training with the weights. The man on the right is Tommy Nobis, All-American and All-Professional guard. (Photograph courtesy of Burnham)

	Sets	Reps.
Quadriceps Extension	2	12
Hamstring Curls	2	12
Leg Press	2	15

Additional specialized exercises for each position may be added if the athlete desires. A good deal of running is also required.[3]

The University of Oklahoma football players train twice a week during the in-season.[4] Their program is as follows:

	Monday		Thursday	
	Sets	Reps.	Sets	Reps.
Power Clean	3	1–6	2	3–8
Full Squat	3	1–6	2	3–8
Bench Press	3	1–6	2	3–8
Leg Extensions	2	8–10	2	10–15
Leg Curls	2	8–10	2	10–15
Neck Machine	1	10–12	1	10–12

The Anaheim Rams have their players train for maximal strength during the off-season. During the in-season they train twice a week, using 60 percent of their maximum to maintain their strength. Bench presses, curls, shoulder shrugs, and squats are emphasized. A study by Willet[5] indicates that an in-season weight-training program of 15 minutes duration, conducted twice weekly, is sufficient to maintain the strength of intercollegiate football players during the in-season.

The training routines described above would probably be improved if more emphasis were placed on neck exercises. The frequency of neck injuries in football is often blamed on the fragility of the first and second cervical vertebrae. It seems an elementary precaution to strengthen the muscles guarding this vulnerable area.

Medical authorities believe that it is important to maintain a strength ratio of 60/40 between the knee extensors and flexors. Some trainers argue that if the ratio reaches 70/30, hamstring pulls become almost a certainty. This implies that conditioning programs should pay more attention to strengthening the hamstrings.

Baseball

The case for the use of weight training in baseball and the principles to be followed in devising such a regimen have been presented by Stallings.[6] Those considering introducing such a program will find his discussion decidedly informative.

Edwards[7] has worked out a set of movements specific for baseball. They include: (1) trunk rotation—arms held out to the sides on line with the shoulders, a six-to-ten-pound dumbbell in each hand; body twisted as far as possible to one side and then to the other; (2) one-hand swing—an eight-or-ten-pound dumbbell held at the opposite shoulder and swung across the chest as if batting; (3) wrist curls—done standing with the forearms parallel to the ground; (4) triceps extension; (5) wrist abductor.

Rada and Chilakos[8] suggest an off-season training program designed to put stress on the muscles used in throwing and batting. Their recommended exercises include shoulder shrugs done in the supine position on a bench, military presses, wrist curls, sit-ups, bent arm lateral raises, wrist abduction, wrist adduction, half-squats, and bent arm pull overs. They prefer the double progressive system practiced three times a week.

Basketball

This basic off-season weight-training program at the University of Kentucky[9] is quite simple:

	Sets	Reps.
Squats	5	5
Power Clean	5	5
Incline Bench	5	5
Step-up on 24″ Bench	2	10
Leg Curl	3	10
Leg Extension	3	10
Toe Raises on Calf Machine	3	12

The program also includes a good deal of interval running.

TV commentators and newspaper reporters have frequently commented on the importance of upper body strength and the obvious lack of it in some of the players—a hint to those responsible for strength development in basketball players.

Judo

The following program is used by students of judo who attend the Kodokan.[10] It is of particular interest because of its stress on the use of dumbbells. Perhaps this has resulted from the fact that Japanese studies have shown that the top judoka were lacking in back and arm strength. The exercises include: (1) squat, (2) dumbbell straight-arm pull-over, (3) heel raise, (4) dumbbell press on bench, (5) flying motion, (6) dumbbell rowing, (7) barbell curl, (8) standing barbell triceps extension, (9) seated dumbbell press behind neck, (10) sit-ups.

A number of alternate programs are presented by Ishikawa and Draeger.[11] These experts recommend that a schedule of three sets of ten repetitions each be followed.

Swimming

Weight training has been popular with swimming coaches for nearly half a century, but the number of styles, distances, etc., make it impossible to discuss the subject in detail here. For a basic series of exercises one might consider the program designed by Homola[12] to develop the muscles and flexibility desirable in this sport. He emphasizes that they must be performed through the full range of movement. His program consists of the following: (1) pull down on a lat machine, (2) bent over rowing motion, (3) dumbbell extensions, lateral raises, and rowing motions while prone on a bench, (4) squats, (5) stiff arm and bent arm pullovers, (6) supine lateral raises on a bench, (7) decline bench presses, (8) iron boot alternate leg raises while supine on an incline bench, and backward raises while prone, (9) isometric scissors exercise against a partially inflated inner tube, (10) donkey toe raises, (11) stiff-leg deadlifts, and (12) side bends with a dumbbell. He suggests eight to ten repetitions and working up from a single set to three sets. Two or three exercise periods a week are recommended.

Tennis

Although power has been shown to have a high correlation to various factors in tennis, there are few studies using weight training as a means of developing power in tennis players. Lew Hoad,[13] however, gives it a good deal of credit for his success. He prefers six exercises, all done with a dumbbell: (1) wrist curls, (2) reverse wrist curls, (3) dumbbell is held with the hand in the midposition. The weight is extended to the right as far as possible and then to the left as far as possible. This is a variation of the wrist curl exercise. (4) Curl. (5) Weight is held horizontally out in front. After a few seconds it is raised to the vertical position. The dumbbell is then returned to the horizontal position. Hoad prefers ten repetitions of each exercise, using as much weight as one can handle.

It must be recognized that this is a highly specialized program, not one designed for the player who needs to increase overall muscular strength and power. The writer would suggest that for the latter a suitably designed circuit might well be the procedure of choice.

Billie Jean King recommends the use of high repetitions to develop strength in muscles around the joints so they will protect the joints. Is her recommendation consistent with her goal?

Track and Field

Like swimming, track and field events are so varied that no booklet of this size can present a reasonable summary of proposed programs for each one. In addition training schedules have become highly complex. At the University of Oregon for instance, the strength development program for sprinters is divided into five separate phases. For the record, the basic strength development phase includes five basic exercises: the bench press, half squat, curls, leg extension, and press behind the neck, and an additional supplementary set of exercises consisting of two abdominal exercises of the runner's choice, leg curls, toe raises, standing lateral raises, and parallel bar dips.[14]

Berger[15] has proposed the following off-season program for the conditioning of track men in general: (1) curl, (2) bench press, (3) one-third squat, (4) upright rowing, (5) sit-up, (6) leg curl with iron boot, (7) forward bend with barbell behind neck, (8) heel raise, (9) press, (10) side bend with barbell on shoulders, (11) wrist curl, (12) knee extension in seated position. He does not recommend this for use during the season as he believes that the fatigue which results from its practice may distract from the development of sports skills.

Weight training is especially popular among the weight throwers. Gary Gubner in effect had a choice of participating in the 1964 Olympic Games as a shot-putter or as a weight lifter and Al Feuerbach (fig. 9.3) was the AAU shot put and weight-lifting champion in 1974. The following program was used by Jay Silvester, at that time the best shot put and discus thrower in the world: (1) clean and jerk, (2) dead lift, (3) bench press, (4) jumping squats, (5) lateral raises on an incline board, (6) triceps extension, (7) press on an incline board, (8) sit-ups. His program was of the light and heavy variety. He lifted three days a week during the off-season and two or three days a week during the competitive season.

John P. Jesse, who had considerable success working with weight throwers and other athletes in Southern California, believed that training programs for the former should stress the development of power in the hamstrings, lower back, abdomen, serratus anterior, hands, and fingers. In his opinion too many weight throwers make the mistake of attempting to gain tremendous overall strength while actually neglecting the muscles most important for success in thier particular sport.

Figure 9.3
Al Feuerbach. In 1974 this athlete was National AAU shot put and 242 lb. weight-lifting champion. Los Angeles Times photo.

Wrestling

Bill Farrell, coach of the highly successful 1972 United States Olympic Wrestling Team, considers his emphasis on weight training one of the principal reasons why his team was so outstanding.[16] He recommends the wrestler train with weights three days a week although 48 hours should elapse between the last tough workout and competition. He divides his program into a Power Section consisting of

	Set No.	Repetitions
Power Clean	1	8
	2	5
	3	3
	4	1
Half Squats	1	10
	2	6
	3	2
Dead Lifts	1	10
	2	6
	3	2

Figure 9.4
William Pearl, Mr. America 1953 and four times amateur or professional Mr. Universe. He won the U.S. Navy wrestling championship and was a first alternate on the 1962 Olympic wrestling team. (Photograph courtesy of Pearl & Stern)

and a General Strength Section. This is based on Circuit Training and includes three tours of the following stations:

		Repetitions
1.	Alternate Dumbbell Press	8–12
2.	Bent Over Rowing	8–12
3.	Knee Extensions	15–20
4.	Alternate Dumbbell Curls	8–12
5.	Neck Extensions	8–12
6.	Back Extensions	8–12
7.	Knee Flexion	15–20
8.	Pull Downs	8–12
9.	Toe Raises	15–20
10.	Triceps Dip with Weight	8–12
11.	Neck Flexion	8–12

Van Vliet[17] has proposed an out-of-season weight-training routine for high school wrestlers. He recommends the following exercises: (1) sit-ups with weight held behind head, (2) two arm reverse curl, (3) high pull-up, (4) bench press, (5) straight arm pull downs, (6) leg press (squat may be substituted if leg press machines are not available), (7) press, (8) bent over rowing, (9) dead lift, (10) two arm curl, (11) bridge, holding weight on chest, (12) bent arm pull over. According to Van Vliet the wrestlers should start with eight repetitions and work up to fifteen. He suggests that they train three times a week and perform three sets of each exercise.

Figure 9.5
Lloyd "Red" Lerille, Mr. America 1960, was undefeated during three seasons of high school wrestling and was runner-up in the All-Navy championships.

Both Bill Pearl (fig. 9.4) and "Red" Lerille (fig. 9.5) were amateur wrestlers before becoming Mr. Americas.

Weight-training programs for athletes should be designed according to the demands of the particular athletic event. Choose a sport and then plan a program suitable for off-season practice. In setting up your program, consider the relative demands for strength and power of the shoulders, chest, abdomen, hamstrings, quadriceps, calves, back, biceps, and triceps.

Summary

Remember training is specific. The more closely a weight-training movement simulates an actual movement of the sport, the more helpful it is likely to be. An example might be the use of a dumbbell with the weight at one end (p. 71) used to strengthen the forearm and wrist of a tennis player. The reader can design his own program by determining which muscles are the most important in a given sport and then using the Muscle Chart (pp. 96–97) as a guide to effective exercises for those muscles. Those requiring more detailed information are referred to a booklet published by the University of Nebraska.[18] This provides a training schedule for both male and female athletes in nearly every intercollegiate sport.

REFERENCES

1. Pierson, William, R. and Philip J. Rasch. 1965. Strength Development and Performance Capacity. *Journal of the Association for Physical and Mental Rehabilitation.* January–February, 17 *et seq.*

2. Jesse, John P. 1979. Misuse of Strength Development Programs in Athletic Training. *Physician and Sportsmedicine.* October, 7:46–52.

3. Marks, Mike. 1980. Summer Football Training at the University of Alabama. *National Strength Coaches Association Journal.* March–April, 2:10–13.

4. Lester, Chuck and Warren Harper. 1978. University of Oklahoma In-Season Football Weight Program. *National Strength Coaches Association Newsletter/Journal.* June–July, 1:15.

5. Willet, James E. 1976. The effects of an in-season weight training program on the muscular strength of intercollegiate football players. Unpublished M.S. thesis, South Dakota State University.

6. Stallings, Jack. 1966. The case for weight training in baseball. *Scholastic Coach.* February, 35:32 *et seq.*

7. Edwards, Donald K. 1965. Strength building program for baseball. *Athletic Journal,* February, 45:12 *et seq.*

8. Chilakos, A. Art and Roger Rada. 1972. Weight training for baseball. *Athletic Journal,* February, 52:14 *et seq.*

9. Etcheberry, Pat. 1980. Kentucky basketball. *National Strength Coaches Association Journal,* March–April, 2:22–23.

10. Draeger, Donn. 1960. Weight lifting for judo. *Strength & Health,* June.

11. Ishikawa, Takahiko and Donn E. Draeger. 1962. *Judo Training Methods: A Sourcebook.* (Rutland, Vt.: Charles E. Tuttle Co., Ind.) pp. 130–137.

12. Homola, Samuel. 1966. Weight training for speed swimmers. *Swimming World,* January, 7:6 *et seq.*

13. Hoad, Lew. 1975. Lew Hoad tells you how to put more power in your game. *Tennis,* September 11:63–65.

14. Whitby, Dennis. 1980. Oregon track strength and conditioning for sprinting. 1980. *National Strength Coaches Association Journal,* May–June, 2:18–19.

15. Berger, Richard A. 1963. Strength training for track and field. *Athletic Journal,* February, 43:50 *et seq.*

16. Driedzic, Stan and Bill Farrell. n. d. USA national weight training and conditioning for wrestling–Part III. *National Strength Coaches Association Journal,* 1:16–19.

17. Van Vliet, George A. 1965. Proposed weight training program for high school wrestlers. Unpublished Master's Thesis, University of Southern California.

18. Epley, Boyd. 1972. *The Strength of Nebraska.* (Lincoln: University of Nebraska.)

Appendix 1
Superficial Muscles
of the Human Body

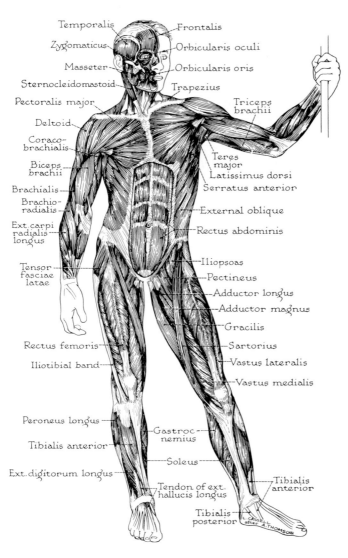

Temporalis
Frontalis
Zygomaticus
Orbicularis oculi
Masseter
Orbicularis oris
Sternocleidomastoid
Trapezius
Pectoralis major
Triceps brachii
Deltoid
Coraco-brachialis
Teres major
Biceps brachii
Latissimus dorsi
Brachialis
Serratus anterior
Brachio-radialis
External oblique
Ext. carpi radialis longus
Rectus abdominis
Tensor fasciae latae
Iliopsoas
Pectineus
Adductor longus
Adductor magnus
Gracilis
Rectus femoris
Sartorius
Iliotibial band
Vastus lateralis
Vastus medialis
Peroneus longus
Gastroc-nemius
Tibialis anterior
Soleus
Ext. digitorum longus
Tibialis anterior
Tendon of ext. hallucis longus
Tibialis posterior

Figure A.1

Superficial Muscles of the Human Body, Anterior View. From B. G. King and M. J. Showers, *Human Anatomy and Physiology*, 5th ed. Copyright © 1953 W. B. Saunders Company, Philadelphia, PA.

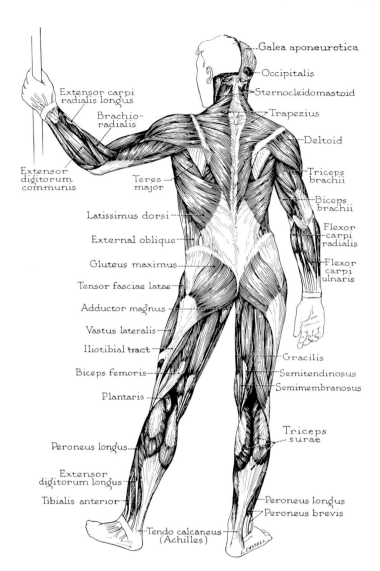

Galea aponeurotica
Occipitalis
Sternocleidomastoid
Trapezius
Deltoid
Triceps brachii
Biceps brachii
Flexor carpi radialis
Flexor carpi ulnaris

Extensor carpi radialis longus
Brachio-radialis
Extensor digitorum communis
Teres major
Latissimus dorsi
External oblique
Gluteus maximus
Tensor fasciae latae
Adductor magnus
Vastus lateralis
Iliotibial tract
Biceps femoris
Plantaris
Peroneus longus
Extensor digitorum longus
Tibialis anterior

Gracilis
Semitendinosus
Semimembranosus
Triceps surae
Peroneus longus
Peroneus brevis
Tendo calcaneus (Achilles)

Figure A.2
Superficial Muscles of the Human Body, Posterior View. From B. G. King and M. J. Showers, *Human Anatomy and Physiology*, 5th ed. Copyright © 1953 W. B. Saunders Company, Philadelphia, PA.

Appendix 2
Muscle Actions
and Exercises

Summary of Muscle Actions and Most Effective Exercises

Muscle	Principal Function	Most Effective Exercises
Abdominis obliquus	Flexion of trunk, flexion to same side, rotation to opposite side	Side bending while holding weight in one hand, twisting sit-ups and leg raises, body twists with barbell on shoulders
Abdominis rectus	Flexion of spine	Sit-ups, vee-ups
Biceps brachii	Flexion and inward rotation of forearm	All forms of curls, reverse curls, and supination-pronation movements
Biceps femoris	Extends thigh, flexes knee	Squats, leg presses, leg curls, and leg backward raises with iron boot
Brachialis	Principal flexor of elbow	All forms of curls and reverse curls
Brachioradialis	Flexion of elbow	*See* Biceps brachii
Deltoid	Three-part muscle; part 1 performs horizontal flexion; part 2, abduction; part 3, horizontal extension	All overhead lifts, side and front raises
Erector spinae	Extension of trunk	Dead lifts, good morning exercise, swan exercise, side bends, dead lifts
Extensor carpi radialis	Extension and abduction of wrist	Reverse wrist curls, wrist abduction exercise

Muscle	Principal Function	Most Effective Exercises
Extensor carpi ulnaris	Extension and adduction of wrist	Reverse wrist curls, wrist adduction exercise
Flexor carpi radialis	Flexion and abduction of wrist	Wrist curls, wrist abduction exercise
Flexor carpi ulnaris	Flexion and adduction of wrist	Wrist curls, wrist adduction exercise
Gastrocnemius	Extends foot; aids in flexing knee	Heel raises, donkey raises in regular and inverted positions, walking on toes with barbell on shoulders
Gluteus maximus	Extension and outward rotation of thigh	Squat, backward leg extenion with iron boot, outward rotation of leg with iron boot
Latissimus dorsi	Draws arms downward, backward, and inward	Lat machine, rowing motion, pull-over
Pectoralis major	Two-part muscle; part 1 functions in arm flexion and abduction; part 2, in arm extension and adduction	Pull-over, flying motion, bench press
Pronator quadratus	Pronates forearm	Pronation-supination of wrist
Quadriceps femoris	Extends knee	Squat, leg press, forward raise of leg, and seated knee extension with iron boot
Rectus femoris	Extends knee and flexes thigh; part of quadriceps femoris	*See* Quadriceps femoris
Rhomboids	Adduct scapula	Rowing motion, shoulder shrugs
Semimembranosus and semitendinosus (hamstrings)	Extends thigh and flexes knee	Squats, leg presses, leg curls with iron boots, backward leg raises
Serratus anterior	Abduction of scapula	All overhead lifts, lateral raise, pull-over
Soleus	Extends foot	*See* Gastrocnemius
Sternocleidomastoid	Flexes and rotates head	Bridging, use of weights suspended from head strap

Muscle	Principal Function	Most Effective Exercises
Supinator	Supinates forearm	Supination-pronation exercise
Supraspinatus	Arm abduction	All overhead lifts, front and side raises
Teres major	Same as latissimus dorsi	*See* Latissimus dorsi
Trapezius	Elevates shoulders and abducts scapula	Shoulder shrugs, all overhead lifts, dead lifts
Triceps brachii	Extension of elbow joint	Overhead lifts, bench presses, French press
Vastus intermedius, internus, and medialis	Parts of quadriceps femoris	*See* Quadriceps femoris

Appendix 3
Glossary

Abduction.
Movement away from the center line of the body.

Adduction.
Movement toward the center line of the body.

Anabolic steroids.
Synthetic hormones believed to promote growth of protein tissue.

Body composition.
Fat weight + lean weight. Exercise decreases fat weight and increases lean weight, thus changing the percentage of each in the body.

Clean and jerk.
An Olympic lift in which the weight is taken to the chest in one movement and then thrown overhead in a second movement.

Cuts.
The separations seen between groups of muscle fibers in exercisers who have participated in intensive training producing a high degree of muscular definition.

Elastic rebound exercise.
An exercise technique in which flexion is followed immediately by extension. The purpose is to use the elastic energy stored when stretching the contracted muscle. If there is a delay between flexion and extension, this energy is lost as heat.

Endocrine glands.
Glands which secrete a substance that affects another organ or part of the body.

Hormones.
Chemical substances which can alter the functional activity of an organ of the body.

Hypertrophy.
Enlargement in the size of a muscle. Increases in hypertrophy are not necessarily closely related to increases in strength.

Isokinetic.
Constant motion; an isotonic contraction in which the speed of movement remains steady.

Isometric.
Constant length; a contraction in which there is no apparent change in angles of the bony levers.

Isotonic.
Constant tension; a contraction in which the angles between the bony levers change.

Lean body weight.
Weight of the lean body mass, including water, mineral, and organic substances. This is not fat-free weight, since it includes the weight of essential fat.

Negative exercise.
A form of isotonic exercise in which the muscle lengthens rather than shortens. Also called eccentric exercise.

Plyometrics.
Exercises in which a concentric contraction immediately follows a quick, forceful eccentric movement. The purpose is to invoke the stretch mechanism—that is, to reinforce the contraction by exciting more motor neurons, and to exercise the muscle eccentrically as well as concentrically.

Power clean.
An exercise in which a weight is taken from knee level to the shoulders in one movement. In the pull stage, the lifter goes up on the toes and then bends at the knees to be able to snap the weight onto the chest.

Prone.
Face downward. The bench press is often erroneously termed the prone press. A true prone press would be a push-up.

Snatch.
An Olympic lift in which a weight is raised overhead in a single movement.

Sticking point.
The point in a lift at which the greatest effort is required in order to complete the movement. This occurs at the joint angle at which the mechanical efficiency is least advantageous.

Supine.
Face up.

Synergistic action.
Simultaneous contraction of two or more muscles to produce a desired action accomplished by neutralizing each other's undesired action.

Appendix 4
Selected References

The following list of supplemental readings is presented for the guidance of the serious weight trainer who desires a more complete understanding of the scientific facts underlying this form of training than is possible to present in this booklet. Articles cited in the text are not included.

Anonymous. August 1985. Home exercise equipment. *Consumer Reports* 50:448–54.

Virginia Aronson. May 1986. Protein and Other Ergogenic Aids. *Physician and Sportsmedicine* 16:199–202.

David H. Clarke. 1973. Adaptations in Strength and Muscular Endurance Resulting from Exercise. In Jack H. Wilmore, ed. *Exercise and Sport Sciences Review.* New York: Academic Press. I:73–102.

Steven J. Fleck, and William J. Kraemer. March-June 1988. Resistance Training. *Physician and Sports Medicine* 16:160–71, 108–24, 63–73, 69–81.

Herbert A. Haupt, and George D. Rovere. November-December 1984. Anabolic Steroids: A review of the literature. *American Journal of Sports Medicine* 12:469–84.

James F. Hickson. October-November 1984. Energy cost of weight training exercise. *National Strength & Conditioning Association Journal* 6:22 *et seq.*

Craig Jensen, and Clayne R. Jensen. August 1978. Update on Strength Training. *Scholastic Coach* 48:90–100.

D. N. Kulund, *et al.* November 1978. Olympic Weight-Lifting Injuries. *Physician and Sportsmedicine* 6:111–19.

G. H. McGlynn. November 1971. A re-evaluation of Isometric Strength Training. *British Journal of Sports Medicine* 6:20–21.

National Academy of Sciences. 1980. Recommended Dietary Allowances, 9th rev. ed. Washington, D.C.

National Strength & Conditioning Association. April-May 1985. Use and abuse of anabolic steroids. *National Strength & Conditioning Association Journal* 7:27.

Philip J. Rasch. 1962. An Introduction to the History of Weight Training in the United States. In Frank Sills, ed. Weight Training in Sports and Physical Education. Washington, D.C.: AAHPER, p. 1–14.

Philip J. Rasch, and Roger K. Burke. 1978. Kinesiology and Applied Anatomy, Sixth ed. Philadelphia: Lea & Febiger.

Harold S. Schendel, and Ellington Darden. July 1972. Food Fads in Athletic Training. *Clinical Medicine* 79:31–35.

Terry Todd. June-July 1984. Karl Klein and the Squat. *National Strength & Conditioning Association Journal* 6:26 *et seq.*

Terry Todd. June-July 1985. The myth of the muscle-bound lifter. *National Strength & Conditioning Association Journal* 7:37–41.

David P. Willoughby. 1970. The Super Athletes. New York: A. S. Barnes and Co.

Jack H. Wilmore. 1976. Athletic Training and Physical Fitness. Boston: Allyn and Bacon, Inc.

James E. Wright, and Michael H. Stone. October-November 1985. National Strength & Conditioning Association Statement on Anabolic Drug Use. *National Strength & Conditioning Association Journal* 7:45–59.

Appendix 5
Questions
and Answers

Multiple Choice

1. Scientific studies have shown use of the sauna by weight trainers.
   a. has definite physiological benefits.
   b. is without definite physiological benefits.
   c. is harmful to exercisers. (p. 8)
2. The lifters at York have popularized
   a. the heavy and light system.   c. the set system.
   b. the light and heavy system. (p. 50)
• 3. The physical activity involved in weight training.
   a. makes it an effective means of reducing weight.
   b. causes the exerciser to become hungry so that he or she eats more and becomes fatter.
   c. is not effective in weight reduction unless dietary intake is regulated. (p. 15)
4. In the opinion of some experts, the most effective system for building up the arms is
   a. sets.   b. supersets.   c., super multiple sets. (p. 54)
5. The "Valsalva phenomenon" results from
   a. a sudden rise in blood pressure, followed by a sudden drop.
   b. a sudden drop in blood pressure, followed by a sudden rise.
   c. a sudden and sustained rise in blood pressure. (p. 19)
6. As a rough guide, a beginner may start his curls with
   a. one-quarter of his body weight   c. one-half of his body weight.
   b. one-third of his body weight. (p. 39)
7. The amount of force that a muscle can exert depends on the number and size of its
   a. sarcoplasm.   b. sarcolemma.   c. myofibrils. (p. 3)
8. The PHA System is the opposite of the
   a. rest-pause system.   c. multipoundage system.
   b. blitz system. (p. 53)
• 9. The present trend in set training is
   a. to use lighter weights in each successive set.
   b. to use the same weight in each successive set.
   c. to use heavier weights in each successive set. (p. 53)
10. A man who is pressed for time may prefer to use
    a. the multipoundage system.
    b. a blitz program.   c. a split routine. (p. 54)

11. The condition known as "muscle-bound"
    a. does not exist.
    b. is commonly found among weight trainers.
    c. is found only among men who train incorrectly.   (p. 8)
12. Vigorous exercise
    a. will "sweat out" a cold.
    b. does not have any effect on a cold's progress.
    c. may make a cold worse.   (p. 20)
13. Circuit training is popular with athletes and the military because
    a. it provides cardiorespiratory stress.
    b. it provides muscular stress.
    c. it is quick and simple.   (p. 51)
14. The rest-pause system
    a. is better for the production of strength than of hypertrophy.
    b. is better for the production of hypertrophy than of strength.
    c. is equally good for either hypertrophy or strength.   (p. 53)
15. The most important factor in exercises designed to increase strength is
    a. intensity.   b. duration.   c. frequency.   (p. 4)
16. The Zinovieff or Oxford technique used in rehabilitation work is simply another
    name for the
    a. light and heavy system.   c. multipoundage system.
    b. heavy and light system.   (p. 50)
17. The "good morning" exercise is a variation of the
    a. front raise   b. high pull-up.   c. straight-legged dead lift. (p. 31)
18. The high pull-up is an excellent exercise for the
    a. trapezius.   b. quadriceps.   c. spinae erectoris.   (p. 25)
19. Many experienced weight lifters consider that the basic exercise for the shoulders
    is
    a. the two-arm press.   c. the press off the back of the neck.
    b. the bench press.   (p. 34)
20. The forearm supinators and pronators receive excellent exercise from
    a. the flying motion.   c. the concentration curl.
    b. the Zottman curl.   (p. 71)
21. A typical superset combination might consist of
    a. curls and presses.   c. squats and dead lifts.
    b. supine presses and push-ups.   (p. 54)
22. When a hopper is used, the amount of weight that can be employed
    a. is reduced.   b. remains the same.   c. may be increased.   (p. 56)
23. To assist in preventing blacking out,
    a. hyperventilate before a lift.
    b. stay in the squatting position as short a time as possible.
    c. lift the weight slowly and carefully.   (p. 20)
24. Anabolic steroids
    a. are recommended for the use of weight trainers.
    b. are both harmless and widely used.
    c. may have highly undesirable side effects.   (p. 14)
25. Progressive resistance exercise tends
    a. to reduce flexibility.   c. to increase flexibility.
    b. to have no effect on flexibility.   (p. 9)

26. "Overtraining" will
    a. reduce both performance capacity and the ability to resist infections.
    b. reduce performance capacity, but not the ability to resist infections.
    c. reduce the ability to resist infections, but not performance capacity.　(p. 21)
27. Most of the standardized set of exercises now in general use derive from a book written by
    a. Bob Hoffman.　　　b. Peary Rader.　　　c. Theodor Siebert.　　　(p. 23)
28. The exercise program based on the theory that muscles should be exercised in a large number of different ways is known as
    a. the 1001 exercise system.　　c. the multipoundage system.
    b. the super multiple set system.　　　　　　　　　　　　　　(p. 39)
29. In order to properly evaluate a program, a man should be prepared to stay on it
    a. one month.　　　b. three months.　　　c. six months.　　　(p. 54)
30. Once a certain level of strength is reached, further gains
    a. continue to improve performance.　　c. hinder performance.
    b. do not improve performance.　　　　　　　　　　　　　　(p. 85)
31. A girl complains of being "flat chested." You might suggest she practice
    a. pull-overs, supine presses, flying motions.
    b. half-squats, presses, curls.
    c. high pull-ups, rowing motion, shoulder shrugs.　　　　　　　(p. 44)
32. An excellent exercise for the triceps is the
    a. dumbbell swing.　b. Hise deltoid exercise.　c. dumbbell high pull-up. (p. 69)
33. Muscle in the female has
    a. the same potential for strength development as does that of the male of comparative size.
    b. a lesser potential for strength development.
    c. a greater potential for strength development.　　　　　　　(p. 41)
34. The practice of weight training produces
    a. little improvement in cardiorespiratory function.
    b. moderate improvement in cardiorespiratory function.
    c. great improvement in cardiorespiratory function.　　　　　　(p. 7)
35. The light and heavy system seem best fitted for the production of
    a. strength.　　　b. hypertrophy.　　　c. definition.　　　(p. 50)
36. The PHA System appears best adapted for the production of
    a. hypertrophy and definition.　　c. strength and hypertrophy.
    b. strength and definition.　　　　　　　　　　　　　　(p. 53)
37. Pangamic acid
    a. is a vitamin.
    b. has a well-known chemical structure.
    c. is a food additive.　　　　　　　　　　　　　　　　　(p. 13)
38. The average young woman tends to have calves which are too small. To overcome this you might prescribe
    a. bent over lateral raises and supine lateral raises.
    b. donkey raises and heel raises.
    c. front raises and lateral raises.　　　　　　　　　　　　(p. 44)
39. The program used by judoka training at the Kodokan stresses use of
    a. barbells.　　　b. dumbbells.　　　c. calisthenics.　　　(p. 89)
40. Most individuals can
    a. press less with dumbbells than with barbells.
    b. press the same with dumbbells as with barbells.
    c. press more with dumbbells than with barbells.　　　　　　(p. 66)

41. The goal in the blitz system is to
   a. keep the blood in constant circulation.
   b. keep the blood in a limited area.
   c. avoid any influence on the blood. (p. 50)
42. A friend asks for an effective exercise for the triceps. You might suggest a
   a. bent-arm pull-over. c. French press.
   b. high pull-up. (p. 37)
43. The correlation between the girth of the forearm and the strength of the handgrip is
   a. low. b. moderate. c. high. (p. 37)
44. It is generally agreed that the average individual requires each night about
   a. eight hours of sleep. c. ten hours of sleep.
   b. nine hours of sleep. (p. 9)
45. Jay Silvester, the best combined shot put and discus thrower in the world, uses
   a. a light and heavy program. c. a multipoundage program.
   b. a heavy and light program. (p. 90)
46. Alterations in body composition as a result of weight training are
   a. greater for men than for women.
   b. about the same for both sexes. c. greater for women than for men
   (p. 42)
47. The front raise with dumbbells is particularly beneficial to the
   a. deltoids. b. triceps. c. biceps. (p. 67)
48. Normally a person should work out
   a. three times a week. c. five times a week.
   b. four times a week. (p. 39)
49. However, a man on a split routine might train
   a. four days a week. c. six days a week.
   b. five days a week. (p. 54)
50. A man doing a reverse curl should expect to handle about
   a. one-third as much as he does in the regular curl.
   b. one-half as much as he does in the regular curl.
   c. two-thirds as much as he does in the regular curl. (p. 25)
51. The major portion of the diet should be
   a. protein. b. carbohydrate. c. fat. (p. 12)
52. One of your students desires to exercise his abdominus oblique muscles. You might suggest the
   a. dumbbell swing. c. side bend.
   b. "good morning" exercise. (p. 70)
53. The training program should provide for
   a. short, frequent rest pauses. c. rest pauses whenever fatigue occurs.
   b. long, infrequent rest pauses. (p. 5)
54. In performing dead lifts, it is best to
   a. have both hands facing forward.
   b. have one hand facing forward and one backward.
   c. have both hands facing backward. (p. 30)

True or False

t f 55. The terms "strength" and "power" are interchangeable. (p. 6)
t f 56. The AMA Committee on the Medical Aspects of Sports has con-
          demned the half-squat as "potentially dangerous to the internal and
          supporting structures of the knee joint." (p. 28)

t f 57. Technically, no work is accomplished during isometric exercise, even though the exerciser becomes fatigued. (p. 3)

t f 58. John Jesse believed that a training program for weight throwers should concentrate on the development of tremendous overall strength. (p. 90)

t f 59. The AAU disbars any athlete known to have used drugs. (p. 14)

t f 60. In the PHA system, a sequence consists of five or six exercises arranged in such a way that each affects a different part of the body. (p. 53)

t f 61. The consumption of large quantities of milk is essential to the weight trainer. (p. 13)

t f 62. The rollers, vibrating belts, and similar machines are effective for spot reducing. (p. 8)

t f 63. Muscle girths should be measured before, not after, exercise. (p. 76)

t f 64. To some extent at least, champions are born, not made. (p. 5)

t f 65. Weight training for women is essentially the same as weight training for men. (p. 43)

t f 66. The use of tobacco is detrimental to the development of strength and hypertrophy. (p. 14)

t f 67. The world's strongest men do not normally win physique contests. (p. 78)

t f 68. The athlete may take it as an axiom that "The more strength and hypertrophy, the better." (p. 85)

Completion

69. Nutritionists recommend that the daily diet include (1) *Milk and cheese;* (2) *Meat, poultry, fish, and beans;* (3) *Vegetables and fruit;* (4) *Bread or cereal;* (5) *Fats, sweets, and alcohol.* (p. 12)

70. A minimum of (*22%*) body fat is believed necesssary for stable reproductive ability and maintenance of normal menstrual cycles in the female. (p. 46)

71. To develop work capacity, a weight training program should be supplemented by (*aerobic exercise*) such as (*running*). (p. 9)

72. The key question in any discussion of the development of muscle is, ("*What can you do with them?*") (p. 85)

73. One advantage of circuit training is that it may be (*"biased"*) to give specialized work to certain muscle groups. (p. 51)

74. Muscular contraction may be divided into the following types—(*isotonic, isometric, lengthening.*) (p. 2)

75. The traditional prescription for losing weight is (*low*) resistance and (*high*) repetitions; for gaining weight it is (*high*) resistance and (*low*) repetitions. (p. 15)

76. The disadvantage of going on a strict diet is that one may lose (*muscle tone*) as well as weight. (p. 15)

77. Those who advocate practice of a few heavy exercises for gaining weight emphasize the slogan (*bulk up, train down.*) (p. 16)

78. It has been shown that harm may result from massive doses of vitamins (*A, D, E, K*). (p. 13)

79. Vitamin supplementation may be required in the case of athletes who (*must make weight*) or who (*train very strenuously.*) (p. 13)

80. The bulk craze has caused many bodybuilders to lose sight of the fact that the (*individual measurements must be in proportion.*) (p. 78)

81. Use of the straight-arm lateral raise and the straight-arm pull-over is subject to the objection that (*they may cause deltoid strain or overstretch the elbow joint.*) (p. 29)

82. Static exercises may be hazardous to individuals suffering from (*heart problems.*) (p. 21)

83. The reducing diet must contain sufficient (*vitamins and minerals*), but be relatively low in (*calories.*) (p. 15)

84. The "overload principle" states that (*strength increases in response to repetitive exercise against progressively increased resistance.*) (p. 4)

85. The dangerous point during dead lifting is the period during which the upper body (*is fully flexed.*) (p. 30)

86. The basic principle of isokinetic exercise is (*to provide resistance proportional to the input of muscular force and alterations in skeletal levers throughout the range of motion.*) (p. 2)

87. The general rule for breathing during weight training is to (*inhale*) while contracting the muscles and (*exhale*) while relaxing them. (p. 20)

88. Some of the older weight trainers are prejudiced against the use of dumbbells on the grounds that (*they make a man "stiff"*). (p. 66)

89. The purpose of the "cheat" in a cheating exercise is to (*get the weight past the "sticking point."*) (p. 50)

90. One factor which stands out in all studies of weight training is (*the great individual differences in response to training programs.*) (p. 49)

91. All advanced training methods depend upon the following principle: (*increasing the amount of stress placed upon the body within the given training period.*) (p. 49)

92. The basic principle in the heavy and light system is (*to keep working the muscles against near maximal resistance.*) (p. 50)

93. Some instructors contend that the position assumed in the bent over rowing motion should be avoided because (*the long lever and the weight of the upper body and resistance place a great strain on the lower back.*) (p. 35)

94. In practicing the Zottman curl, the amount of weight that can be handled will be controlled by (*the strength that can be exerted in the reverse curl.*) (p. 71)

95. Too much protein in the diet may leave an (*acid residue*) which throws an extra load on (*the kidneys.*) (p. 12)

96. The rowing motion to the waist appears to have more effect on the (*latissimus dorsi*) muscle than does the rowing motion to the chest. (p. 34)

97. In performing POBNs, it is essential that the weight not be allowed to (*drop on the vertebrae of the neck.*) (p. 34)

98. Chemically and organically grown foods do not differ in (*taste*) or (*chemical analysis.*) (p. 11)

99. If a muscle is worked regularly, the following changes will occur: (*a permanent increase in the number of capillaries; the ability of the muscle to assimilate nutritive materials will improve; the size and functional power of the cells will improve.*) (p. 3)

100. In routine dumbbell training, most trainers seem to prefer (*alternate*) exercises. (p. 66)

Question Answer Key

Multiple Choice

1. b	12. c	23. b	34. a	45. a
2. a	13. a	24. c	35. a	46. b
3. c	14. a	25. c	36. b	47. a
4. c	15. a	26. a	37. c	48. a
5. a	16. b	27. c	38. b	49. c
6. b	17. c	28. a	39. b	50. c
7. c	18. a	29. b	40. a	51. b
8. b	19. c	30. b	41. b	52. c
9. b	20. b	31. a	42. c	53. a
10. c	21. a	32. b	43. b	54. b
11. c	22. c	33. a	44. a	

True or False

55. F	60. T	65. T
56. F	61. F	66. F
57. T	62. F	67. T
58. F	63. T	68. F
59. T	64. T	

Name Index

Subject Index